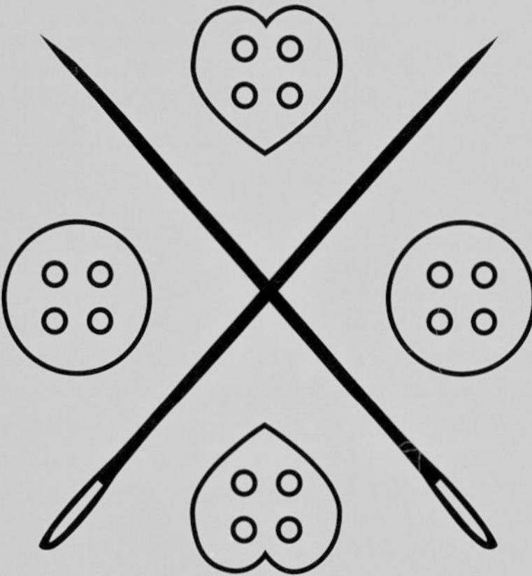

To the makers of the world,
who make stuff, share stuff,
and keep us inspired.

LOVE AT FIRST STITCH

TILLY WALNES

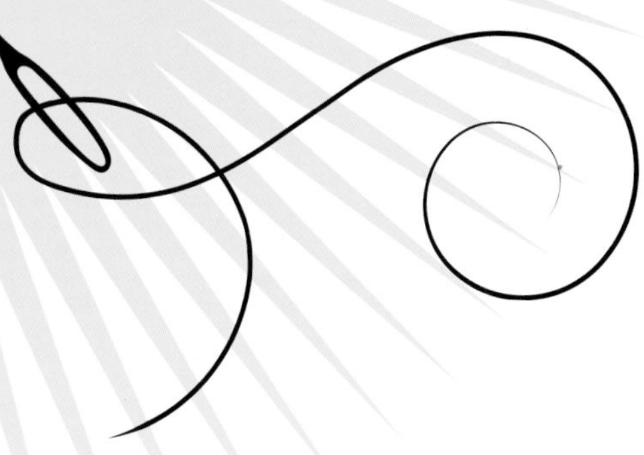

ROOST BOOKS
Boston
2014

CONTENTS

× × ×

GARMENT GALLERY

Brigitte Scarf 18

Brigitte Scarf: variation 34

Brigitte Scarf: variation 36

Margot Pajamas 40

Margot Pajamas: variation 62

Margot Pajamas: variation 61

Delphine Skirt 68

Delphine Skirt: variation 88

Delphine Skirt: variation 86

Megan Dress 92

Megan Dress: variation 110

Megan Dress: variation 112

Clémence Skirt 116

Clémence Skirt: variation 130

Mimi Blouse 138

Mimi Blouse: variation 154

Mimi Blouse: variation 152

Lilou Dress 162

Lilou Dress: variation 174

Lilou Dress: variation 176

. . . DREAMING UP A DRESS IN YOUR HEAD, AND SETTING OUT TO MAKE IT EXACTLY AS YOU ENVISION IT . . .

. . . holding your breath as you make that first daring slice into a fresh piece of fabric . . .

. . . immersing yourself for hours in a magical world of colors, textures, and trimmings . . .

. . . WATCHING THE DRESS OF YOUR DREAMS TAKE SHAPE BEFORE YOUR EYES . . .

THE JOY OF STITCHING IS . . .

. . . KNOWING THAT NO ONE ELSE IN THE WORLD HAS THE SAME OUTFIT AS YOU . . .

. . . realizing you haven't been shopping for clothes in six months . . .

. . . wearing clothing that actually fits your body and that makes you feel good . . .

. . . TAKING PLEASURE IN THE EXPERIENCE OF MAKING SOMETHING WITH YOUR OWN HANDS.

MY STORY

FOUR YEARS AGO I FELT A SUDDEN AND OVERWHELMING URGE TO MAKE SOMETHING.

Like many of us, most of my day involved sitting at a desk, typing on and staring at a computer hour after hour. While I loved my job working with indie cinemas and film festivals, I felt a strong desire to use my hands for a more creative purpose, to produce something tangible, and to reawaken a childlike sense of experimentation and play that I felt I had lost since I became a grown-up.

At the same time, I was wrestling with my conscience over my shopping habits.

I've always loved clothes, and like many people my age, I'd never learned to make them myself. While previous generations of my family were skilled in sewing—from my great-grandfather the Polish East London tailor to my mother, who started her career as a fashion designer—when I was growing up we were more concerned with how to use a computer than a sewing machine. We could buy our clothing so cheaply, so why should we bother making it? Yet consuming ready-made garments left me unsatisfied, and I was experiencing a growing sense of malaise at the environmental impact and ethical implications of my contribution to the high turnover of cheaply made, disposable fashion.

So one day, on a whim, I signed up for a beginner sewing class. A few days and numerous pin injuries later, I was proudly wearing my first homemade dress to a New Year's Eve party, basking in the glory of being able to return compliments with, "Why thank you, I made it myself!" Overnight, I felt creative again, more productive, and my urge to shop had magically vanished. My obsession with dressmaking was born. Over the next few years, I spent most of my waking hours—and much of my dreams—fantasizing about fabrics, scrutinizing stitches, and contemplating construction. I gathered up information through books, blogs, and trial and error. Later on, I consolidated this knowledge by taking courses in professional sewing and pattern drafting at the London College of Fashion. I began designing my own patterns, taking pleasure in the combination of math and drawing, finally able to make the dresses of my daydreams a reality.

I began my blog, *Tilly and the Buttons*, as a way to connect with other dressmaking enthusiasts. I became part of a virtual sewing circle of people across the globe who generously pool knowledge, share skills, collectively problem solve, and inspire each other to keep creating. People read my blog for the same reason I love reading other sewing blogs—I'm no expert tailor who has been stitching since I was in the womb. Rather, I'm an ordinary person, like you, who enjoys making clothes for myself, at home, for fun.

I kept hearing the same story from my blog readers as well as from real-world friends—that they would love to start making their own clothes, but they found the jargon and conventions of traditional sewing resources confusing, or they had had a traumatic experience at school with an intimidating, dogmatic teacher. I found this so sad, as I really wanted other people to discover the pleasure of making clothes with their own hands.

So, combining my passion with my professional background in designing learning programs, I made it my mission to demystify dressmaking for a new audience. Teaching offline and sharing tutorials online, I set about trying to take the head-scratching out of sewing, by translating the jargon, explaining the things that can throw beginners, and stirring it all together with a hearty dose of encouragement. At the same time, my readers were asking me to share my sewing pattern designs, so after a ton of work testing, refining, and creating visual, user-friendly instructions, I began releasing them through my blog. The patterns have become more popular than I ever imagined, and I love seeing photos around the Internet of people proudly wearing the garments they've made from them.

Eventually, as the blog expanded and my inbox overflowed, I made the decision to leave my film-industry career behind me and follow a new dream. Now my full-time job is helping people to start making their own clothes, and I couldn't be happier.

My hope is that this book will help to introduce the joys of dressmaking to a new audience. To an audience who wants to rediscover the pleasures of making; who wants to become less wasteful and more self-reliant; who chooses to celebrate rather than disparage activities historically considered the preserve of women; and who wants to take back control of what they wear by creating it themselves.

This is the book I wish had existed when I started sewing.

Tilly Walnes

HOW TO USE THIS BOOK

If you're new to sewing, the best way to use this book is to start at the beginning and work through it. It will take you from the absolute basics of threading a sewing machine through to being a confident DIY (do-it-yourself) dressmaker with a closet full of gorgeous garments you'll love to wear—step by step, technique by technique, project by project.

Since the best way to learn is to start doing, this book gets you sewing right away. Each chapter is centered around a project—beginning with a simple scarf as you get a grip on stitching, through to an impressive lined dress. Rather than overwhelming you with too many techniques all at once, each chapter teaches you just enough to make the project, building your skills gradually as you progress through the book. After all, no one needs to master five different seam finishes before they can make a dress. The book also explains those things that can really throw beginners—translating the jargon, demonstrating techniques through images, and including extra touches to make it easier to understand, such as pattern pieces with labeled seamlines.

Whether you're a newbie or an experienced stitcher, the garment projects will help you build a handmade wardrobe of gorgeous, contemporary, and wearable designs. They can be made again and again, in whatever prints and colors you favor—whether that's bold colors, earthy tones, pastels, or monochrome. The projects start off simple and gradually become more complex as your skills and confidence grow.

Each chapter's key techniques are on a gridded white background to distinguish them from the project steps on the plain yellow background—so if you want to skip a project, you can still refer to the techniques; or if you're already confident in your skills, you can just follow the project steps to make the garments.

The paper patterns for five of the projects are supplied with this book (the Brigitte Scarf and Clémence Skirt chapters explain how to make the patterns yourself). Each pattern comes in a range of sizes labeled from 1 to 8, and the seam allowances are included on the pieces. I purposely avoid the ready-to-wear sizing system (8, 10, 12, etc.) because it can be misleading since it varies so much between stores and territories. Instead, I encourage you to choose your size(s) by consulting the body measurements and finished garment measurements detailed for each project, and make a garment to fit your unique proportions. Page 47 will help you identify your pattern size and explains how to use the patterns, and page 73 shows you how to combine multiple sizes if necessary.

Part of the joy of sewing is adding your own design flourishes to a garment. The book outlines two bonus variations for each project, as well as listing ideas for other ways to make the garments your own. You can mix and match these ideas to create countless different styles of the projects to go in your handmade wardrobe.

Each chapter also includes musings and tips on the sewing lifestyle, answering common conundrums such as how to squeeze stitching into a busy routine and how to behave in a fabric store. My hope is that this book will inspire you not only to start making your own clothes but to make dressmaking a way of life.

YOU WILL NEED . . .

ESSENTIAL TOOLS

SEWING MACHINE—see page 16 for tips on sourcing your first machine.

PRESSER FEET—regular, zipper, invisible zipper, buttonhole—these attachments may already come with your machine, or if you're buying them separately, make sure they fit your model of machine. (1)

STEAM IRON AND IRONING BOARD—essential for a great-looking finish (page 57).

FABRIC SCISSORS—find a sharp pair that feels comfortable to use and never use them to cut paper or the blades will quickly become blunt. (2)

SEAM RIPPER—keep this by your side to remove any stitching you're not happy with. (3)

TAPE MEASURE—to drape around your neck and pretend you're Coco Chanel. (4)

PINS—long pins with visible glass heads are my personal favorites, plus fine pins for fine fabrics (page 30). (5)

SEWING MACHINE NEEDLES—needles come in different sizes to suit different weights of fabric, ranging from 8/60 for very fine fabrics such as chiffon, through 12/80 for lightweight to medium-weight fabrics such as cotton poplin, up to 18/110 for heavy denim and canvas. For knits, get a ballpoint, or stretch, needle. (6)

HAND-SEWING NEEDLES—for attaching buttons (page 151) and hand finishing. (7)

THREAD—buy a spool or two of all-purpose polyester thread in the same color as your fabric (or, if you can't find an exact match, slightly darker will blend in better than slightly lighter will). Contrasting colors are useful for basting. (8)

MARKING TOOLS—my favorite method of marking fabric involves a tracing wheel, dressmaker's carbon, and cutting mat (page 51). Other great options for marking include tailor's chalk, chalk pencils, washable felt-tip pens, and air-erasable pens whose ink fades over time—awesome. (9)

LARGE PAPER, PENS, PENCILS, PAPER SCISSORS, LONG RULER, CURVED RULER (10), GLUE OR TAPE—for tracing and adjusting paper sewing patterns (page 47).

NICE TO HAVE

SMALL SCISSORS—keep a pair of thread snippers, embroidery scissors, or even nail scissors close by for snipping threads.

MAGNETIC PIN HOLDER—seriously handy for when you drop your pins all over the floor.

TAILOR'S HAM—great for pressing shaped areas such as darts (page 101).

SLEEVE BOARD—brilliant for pressing tubular forms.

ROTARY CUTTER—makes cutting slippery and stretchy fabrics a breeze—just don't forget the cutting mat.

OVERLOCK PRESSER FOOT—helpful for getting your zigzag stitching in the right place.

THREAD WAX—waxing your thread before hand sewing can help prevent pesky knots from forming.

OVERLOCKER—a worthwhile investment for beautifully finished seams a little further down the line (page 56).

4
3
9
9
9
5
7
2
6
8
10
9
9
9
1

SOURCING YOUR FIRST SEWING MACHINE

YOU DON'T HAVE TO SPEND A TON OF MONEY

High-end digital sewing machines can cost thousands, but a beginner can get a decent mechanical model for a reasonable price. When I was first starting out, I got a cheapo model and it served me well for years. You can always upgrade to a more expensive machine in a few years' time.

YOU MIGHT NOT EVEN HAVE TO SPEND ANY MONEY!

Put the word out that you're learning to sew and you may be surprised at just how many people confess to owning an unused machine collecting dust in the attic. You'd be doing them a favor to take it off their hands, *non*? Ask around—friends, aunts, Twitter, charity stores, your local freecycle group. It may need a service at a sewing machine center, but it could save you money while you're testing the waters.

KEEP IT SIMPLE

Don't get overwhelmed by all the functions and stitch types on expensive machines. Unless you're determined to be the queen of decorative topstitching, chances are you're only going to regularly use three stitch types—straight, zigzag, and buttonhole. There's not much point splashing extra cash to get extra stitches you'll never use.

SIZING UP

If you want to sew garments from scratch, I would avoid those little half-size machines, as cute as they look. Pick a full-size machine, strong enough to handle any thicker fabrics you may want to sew with. Sturdy machines often hold strong guts, but if you're sewing on the kitchen table and need to pack away at dinnertime, you may prefer something that's relatively light and portable.

TEST OUT A FEW MODELS

You can buy sewing machines online and from department stores, or a specialty retailer can offer expert advice and even let you try out a few models to see which one you're most comfortable using.

CONSIDER THE BRAND

I'm not a brand snob, but if you get one of the well-known brands of machines you will probably find it easier in the future to get accessories to fit it, or find someone to service or repair it if something goes wrong.

WORK OUT WHAT'S IMPORTANT TO YOU

Some factors you may want to consider:

- Can you thread the machine easily?
- Does it sew buttonholes automatically or manually? Which you choose is personal preference (pages 149–50).
- Does the machine come with any useful accessories, such as a zipper foot?
- Does it make a lot of noise?
- Can it handle the kinds of fabrics you want to sew with?
- Most important, do you feel comfortable using it?

DON'T SWEAT IT!

Whichever machine you choose is going to get you started sewing your dream wardrobe. So don't worry too much about which one to go for—just go for it!

MY SEWING PHILOSOPHY

YOU CAN MAKE SEWING AS EASY OR AS DIFFICULT AS YOU LIKE.

You don't need decades of experience to make clothes that you'll love to wear.

Approach a dressmaking pattern like a blank canvas to create a garment that's unique to you.

AS WITH SO MANY THINGS IN LIFE, THERE IS USUALLY NO SINGLE "CORRECT" WAY OF DOING THINGS. DO WHAT WORKS FOR YOU.

TAKE YOUR TIME AND ENJOY THE PROCESS. SEWING SHOULDN'T BE DONE IN A HURRY.

Don't let the pursuit of perfection hold you back: it probably looks much better than most chain store clothing.

EXPERIMENT, PLAY, AND ENJOY!

BRIGITTE SCARF

CHAPTER 1

Let's get sewing! If you're new to using the sewing machine, this chapter will guide you through the essentials of getting started, from threading your sewing machine to accurate stitching. Then we'll dive into making a super-speedy project. Tie the Brigitte Scarf around your head to channel Bardot and add a touch of Riviera chic to your handmade wardrobe.

SUPPLIES

For practicing stitching:

Unbleached cotton calico fabric OR another light-colored medium-weight cotton fabric

Thread (in a contrasting color so you can easily see your stitches)

For the scarves:

At least 6" x 60" (15 cm x 150 cm) of fabric for the head scarf

OR 32" x 32" (80 cm x 80 cm) of fabric for the square neck scarf variation (page 35)

Thread (in color to match your fabric)

Large sheet of paper

TOOLS

See page 14

OPTIONAL

Contrasting thread for topstitching

TECHNIQUES

Setting up your sewing machine (page 21)

Stitching school (page 26)

Pinning (page 30)

Adjusting stitches (page 32)

FABRIC SUGGESTIONS

Choose a fabric that is lightweight and drapey, such as cotton lawn, voile, or shirting. Lightweight silks, polyesters, and blends will make a beautiful scarf, but their slipperiness can make them tricky to work with if you're just starting to sew—test sew them first if you're unsure. Medium-weight cottons will also work well for the head scarf, but not so well for the square neck scarf variation on page 35.

SETTING UP YOUR SEWING MACHINE

TECHNIQUE

Let's get your sewing machine set up and ready to go. I know how boring it can be to read the super-dry manual that came with your machine, so here is the essential information you need to start sewing. Functions will vary between different models though, and it is important to use your machine safely, so do read the manual at least once and keep it on hand.

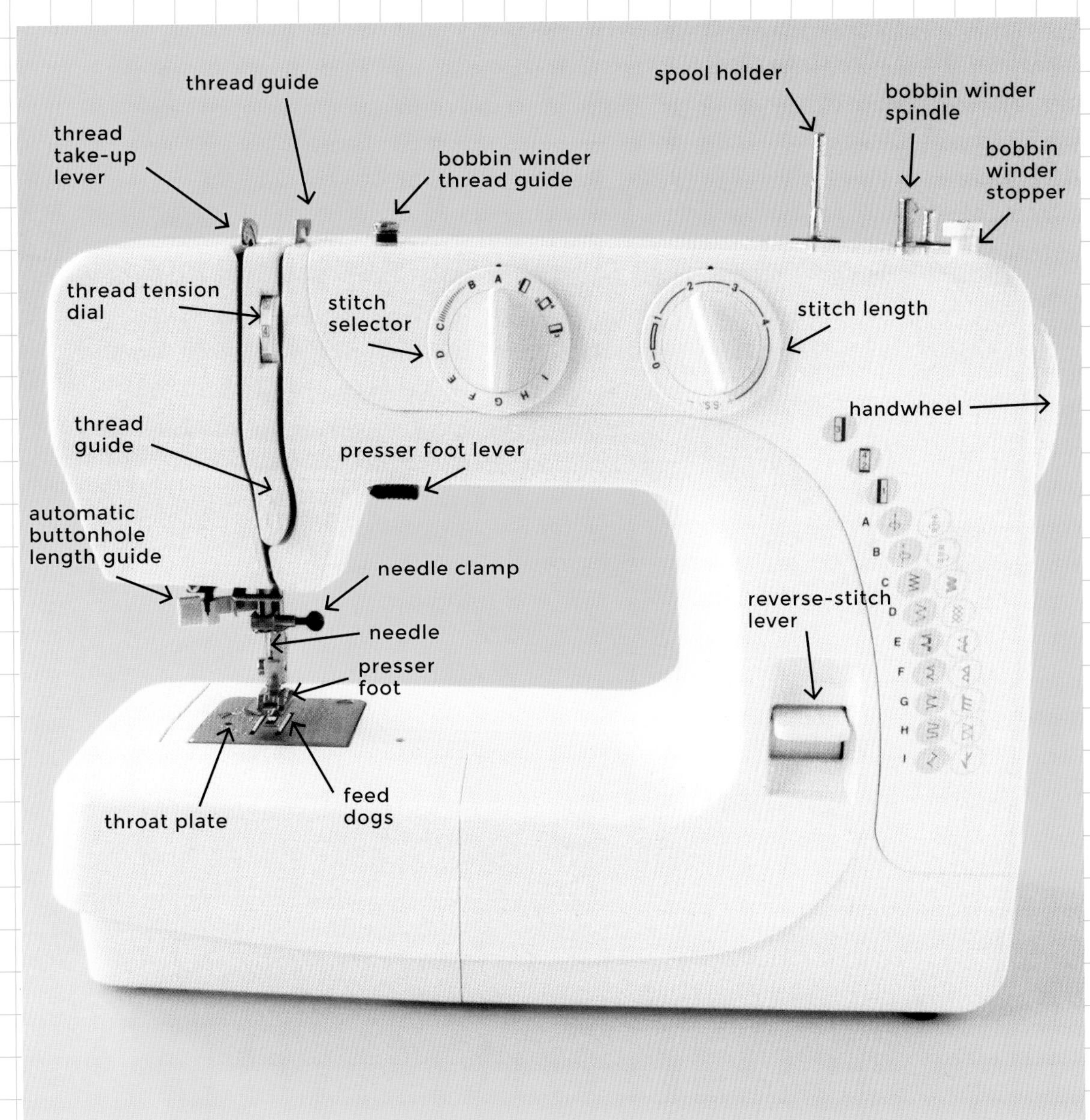

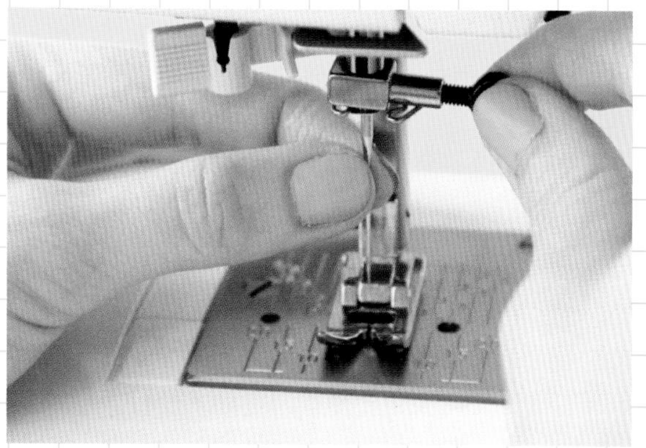

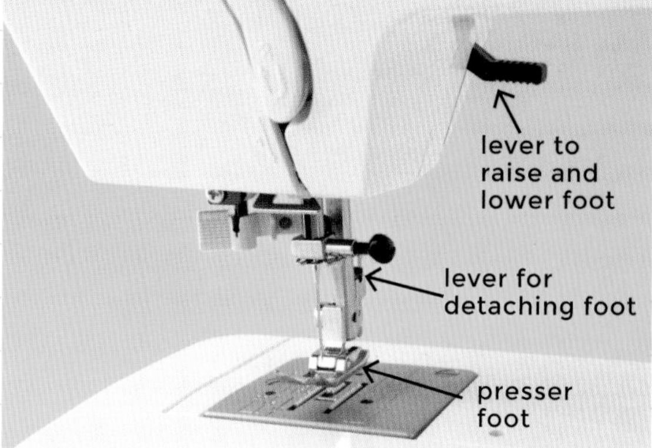

Connect your machine to the power supply using the cord. Plug the foot pedal into the side of your machine and position it on the floor so that it's within comfortable reach of your foot.

CHANGING THE NEEDLE

It's a good idea to change the needle on your sewing machine every few projects to keep it sharp. You'll also want to switch to a different type or size of needle for different kinds of fabrics. To remove the needle, use your fingertips to unscrew the little knob (the needle clamp) on the right-hand side of the needle shaft until the needle is loose enough to pull out. To insert a needle, push it up into the shaft as far as it will go with the flat side of the needle facing toward the back of the machine, then screw in the little knob on the right-hand side of the shaft to secure it in place.

You need to be careful not to accidently press on the foot pedal while you're fiddling with the needle, so make sure the machine is turned off or the pedal is well away from your feet.

ATTACHING THE PRESSER FOOT

Not to be confused with the foot pedal, the presser foot (often shortened to plain old "foot") is the little gizmo that holds the fabric in place while sewing. There's a lever at the back of the machine that allows you to raise the foot to move the fabric or lower the foot to hold the fabric in place. The foot is attached to the bottom of the bar that is behind the needle and—depending on your machine—will either screw or snap on.

If it's a snap-on, to detach the foot you just need to raise it using the lever, then press the small button or lever at the back of the bar and the foot will drop off. To attach the presser foot, position the little pin on the foot directly underneath the little claw on the bar, then lower the lever—you may need to shuffle it about a little until it clicks in place. Raise the lever to check that it's firmly attached and won't fall off.

If it's a screw-on, there will be a little screw on the left-hand side of the bar holding the foot, and a matching screwdriver with the machine's accessories. If the screw needs to come all the way out to change the foot, be very careful not to lose it.

THREADING YOUR SEWING MACHINE

The first time you thread a sewing machine, it can seem insanely complicated, but after a few goes it'll become second nature. It's really worth practicing threading a few times as, once you've cracked this, everything else will be a breeze.

Wind the bobbin

1 The sewing machine creates stitches by weaving together thread from two sources—the spool and the bobbin. The spool of thread sits on top of the machine. The bobbin (don't you just love that word?), which goes inside the machine below the presser foot, is a small reel that comes empty—so you need to transfer some of the thread from the spool to the bobbin before you start sewing.

2 The prong sticking out the top of your machine, either vertically or horizontally, is the spool holder. Place the spool of thread on the spool holder, with the thread coming out from behind and toward the left. Pull out some thread and wrap it halfway around the little silver nubbin on the top left of the machine, officially known as the bobbin winder thread guide or tension disk. Depending on your machine, there may be another thread guide to pass it through first—check your manual if you're not sure. Now insert the thread up through the tiny hole in the top of the bobbin.

3 Keeping hold of the end of the thread, position the bobbin on top of the bobbin winder spindle, and secure it by flicking either the spindle toward the stopper next to it or vice versa, depending on your machine. Switch your machine on and, still holding the thread for the first few seconds, press your foot down on the pedal to wind the thread from the spool onto the bobbin. On some machines, you can pull out the handwheel on the right-hand side of the machine to wind the bobbin without the needle moving up and down. On other models, there is a dedicated bobbin-winding button. Keep winding until the bobbin is full. Cut the thread to detach the spool from the bobbin, then flick the bobbin away from the winder stopper to take it off. You can switch your machine off again now.

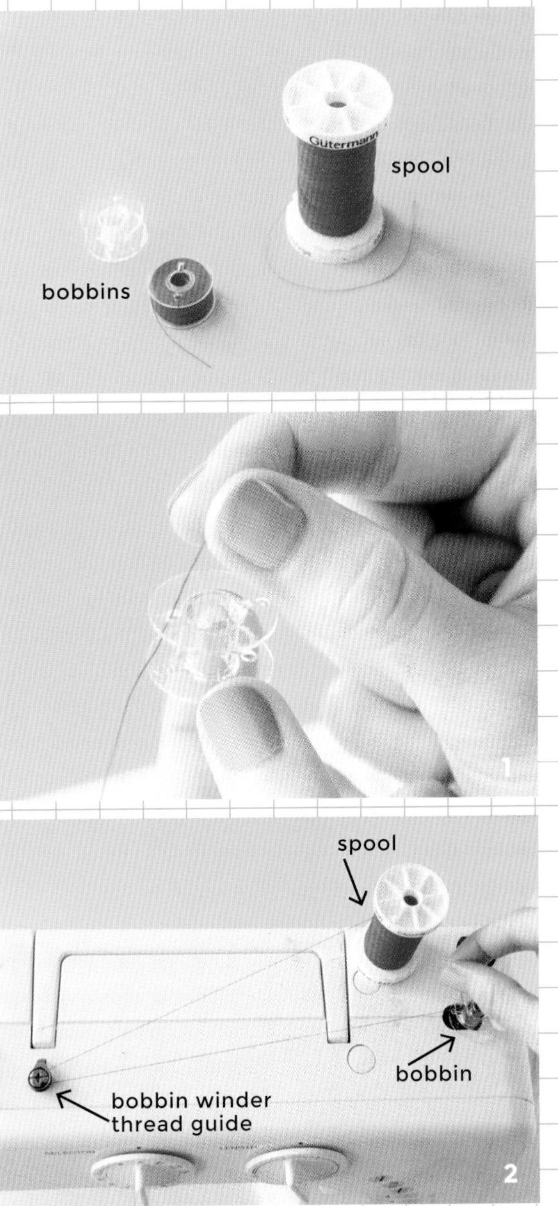

WRONG-WAY WIND

If your thread ends up on the spindle rather than the bobbin, it may have been threaded the wrong way—oops! Unwind it and try again.

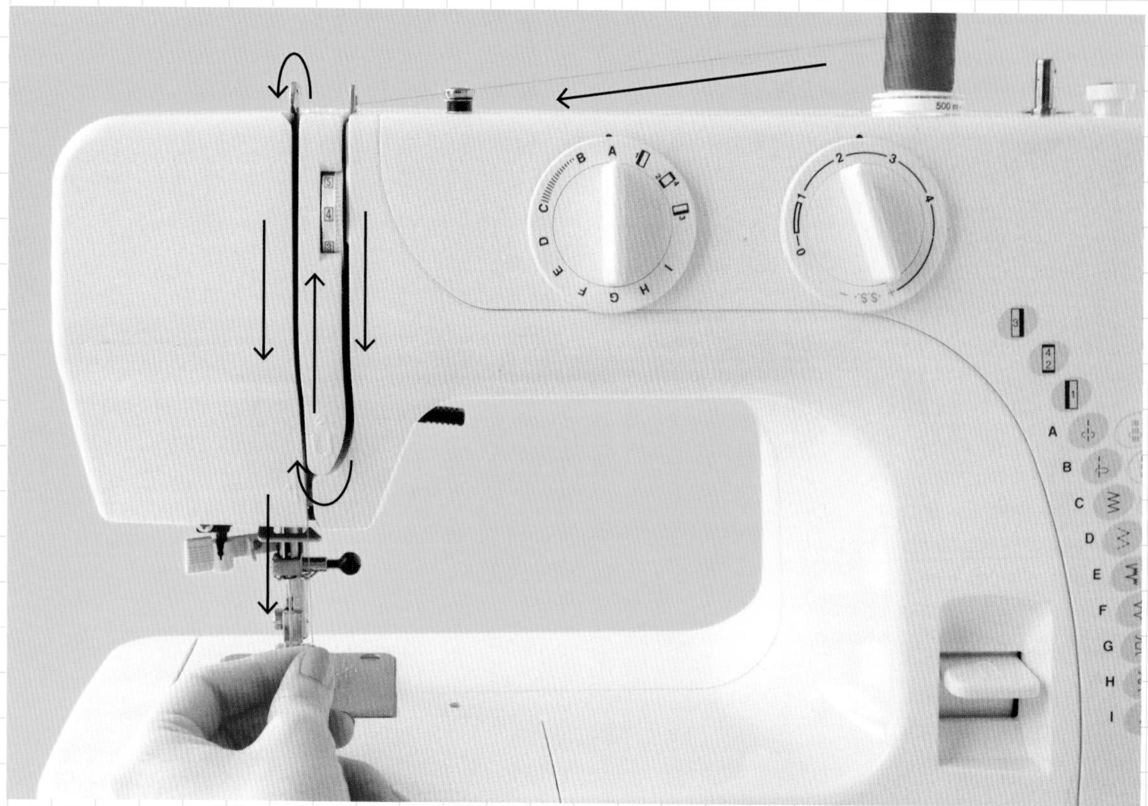

Thread the spool

Now we're ready to begin threading. Your machine may have a diagram printed directly on it to guide you. With the spool still on the spool pin, pull some thread out toward the left, and through any thread guides if your machine has them (check the manual if you're not sure). Draw the thread from right to left around the first hook (thread guide), down the first channel, up the second channel, through the second hook (take-up lever—if you can't see it, use your handwheel to raise it), then back down the second channel.

Draw the thread behind the two hooks above the needle—the larger one toward the front of the machine and a smaller one directly above the needle. Now you can thread the needle itself, from front to back, either by hand or using the automatic needle threader, if there is one and if you're that way inclined. If you find threading the needle tricky, snip the thread so the end is tightly twisted with no fluffy fraying.

Thread the bobbin

The bobbin goes into the bottom of your machine, usually in one of two common ways:

1 **Front-loading machine.** To insert the bobbin into a front-loading machine, you'll usually begin by taking off a removable part of the casing on the bottom left-hand side to leave you with the free arm. Flip down a cover to reveal a metal bobbin case, which you can pull out with a latch. With the bobbin case in your left hand, insert the bobbin with your right, with the thread unwinding in an counterclockwise direction. Pull about 4" (10 cm) of thread through the tiny slit in the side of the case, under the flap and out the little hole. Now place the case back in the machine.

2 **Top-loading machine.** On a top-loading machine, the bobbin goes under the cover plate just in front of the presser foot. Slide the button to the right-hand side of the plate to release it. Place the bobbin in the case below, with the thread unwinding in an counterclockwise direction. Pull about 4" (10 cm) of thread out and through the little slit following the diagram on the cover plate.

3 Now that you've inserted the bobbin, you need to pull the bobbin thread up to the surface of the machine. To do this, you use the spool thread to fish it out and the method is the same no matter what type of machine you have. Holding the end of the spool thread in your left hand, turn the handwheel one full rotation with your right to move the needle all the way down and back up again. Or press the up/down needle position button if your machine has one. Gently tug on the spool thread in your left hand and you should see a loop of bobbin thread emerge. You can use the end of some thread scissors or a pen to pull this loop all the way out. Now close the cover and replace the casing (on a front loader) or the cover plate (on a top loader).

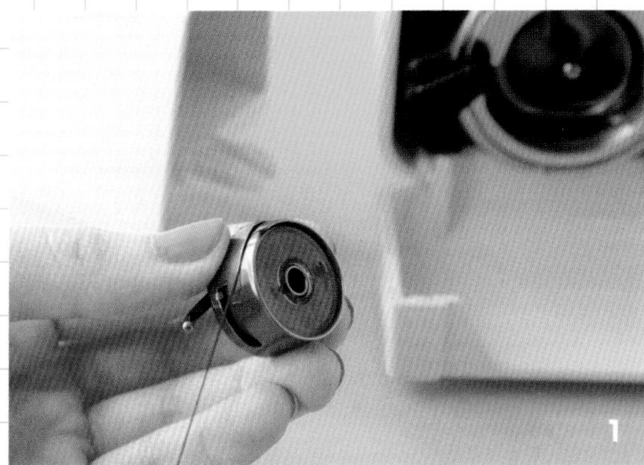

1

2

3

And you've threaded your sewing machine! That seemed like a massive mission, didn't it? I promise you that once you get used to it you'll be able to do the whole thing in a few seconds without even having to think about it. Don't believe me? Unthread it and try again. And again. Show that machine who's boss!

STITCHING SCHOOL

TECHNIQUE

Now comes the fun part—let's start stitching! Grab some light-colored cotton fabric (such as unbleached calico) to practice on, and thread the machine with some bright-colored thread so your stitches are easy to see.

PREPARING TO STITCH

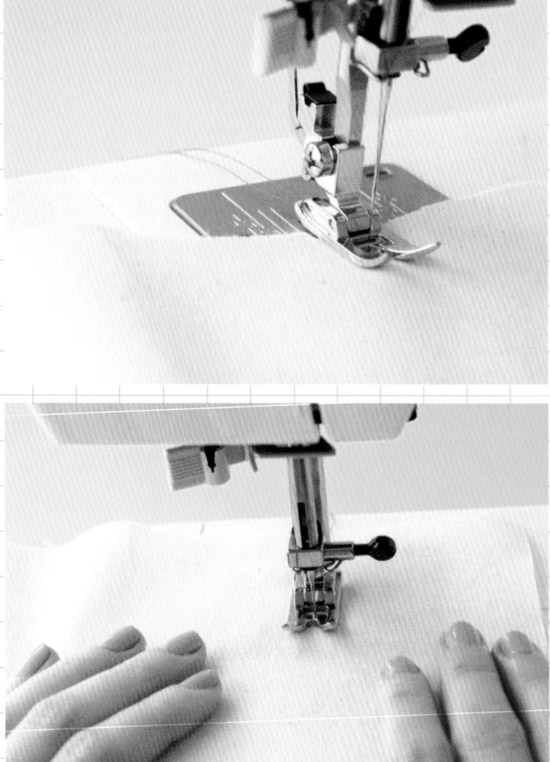

Set your stitch length to 1⁄16–1⁄8" (1.5–3 mm), using the stitch length knob or button. With the needle in the highest position (use the handwheel to move it if it's down), pull out about 4" (10 cm) of thread from both spool and bobbin toward the back of the machine—this will help prevent the threads from unraveling when you start the machine. Place the fabric under the presser foot (raise it with the lever if it's down) and thus sandwiched between spool and bobbin threads. You'll be moving the fabric away from you as you sew, so the fabric should be in front of the machine, with 1⁄8" (3 mm) or more behind the needle so the threads don't get knotted up around each other. Lower the presser foot to hold the fabric in place.

GO!

Switch the machine on. Place your hands on the fabric on either side of the needle (but not too close!) to help gently guide the fabric, without pushing or pulling on it. Lower your foot onto the pedal and start stitching . . . Woooooooooooooooop!

Soooo much fun. And no, it never gets old.

SPEED CONTROL

Some sewing machines have a speed setting; if you're so inclined, you can begin cautiously and build up to turbo power. Otherwise, adjusting the speed is a case of learning to control the amount of pressure you put on the pedal—it can take practice to get it right, but you'll have a hoot in the process.

For super precision, you can manually turn the handwheel on the right-hand side of your machine toward you to make a stitch. This is really useful if you just want to create one or two stitches; for example, if you're trying to end your stitching at a particular point.

CUTTING LOOSE

Once you've finished stitching, raise the presser foot and pull out your fabric (if you're finding that your fabric won't budge, try raising the needle with the handwheel). Snip the threads using either small scissors or—if your machine has one—the nifty little cutter tucked away on the left-hand side of your machine. Awesome. It's good to get into the habit of snipping your threads close to the fabric so you don't end up with any random tails on your finished outfits.

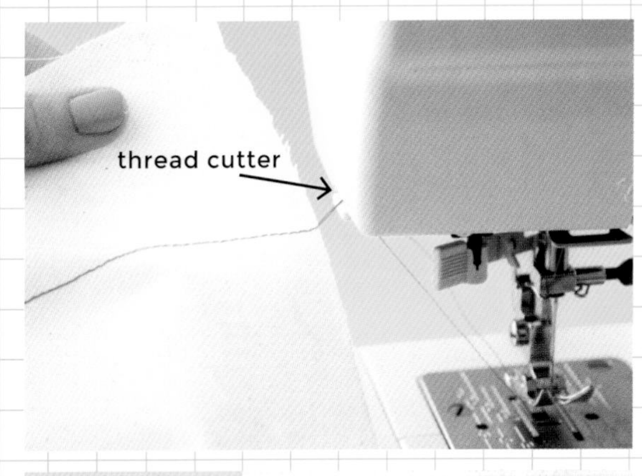

BACKSTITCHING

Unless you're creating temporary stitches (such as basting stitches), you'll want to secure them to keep them from unraveling. To do this, sew two or three stitches backward—known as "backstitching" or "reverse stitching"—over the beginning and end of each line of stitching. Your machine will have a button or a lever, often labeled with a turning arrow, which you can hold down while you're sewing to stitch backward. So when you start a line of stitching, go forward two or three stitches, then backward two or three stitches, then sew the full line before finally reversing again for two or three stitches.

If you've sewn off the end of the fabric, you can tie the threads together into a double knot by hand. This is useful on the point of a dart for example, where backstitching would cause unsightly bulk.

backstitching

STITCHING LINES

Ready to get serious? Let's practice precision stitching. Draw some straight lines and curvy lines on your fabric. Now stitch directly over the lines as accurately as you can. Keep an eye on the part of the line directly in front of the needle, and use your hands to gently guide the fabric in the right direction. Go as slowly or as quickly as feels right, and take as many pauses as you need to.

Don't worry if it looks like a total mess first time around—that's normal! Have a few goes and you'll see your stitching improve quickly.

NEEDLE DOWN

If you want to pause in the middle of a line of stitching, try to stop with the needle down in the fabric; some machines can be set to do this automatically. That way you can't accidently shift the fabric under the presser foot before you start stitching again.

STITCHING CORNERS

As well as stitching in straight lines and curves, occasionally you'll need to turn a sharp corner. Draw a large corner onto your fabric to practice. Start stitching from one end, stopping with your needle down in the fabric exactly on the point of the corner—you can turn the handwheel to get to the right place. Now raise the presser foot and pivot the fabric so the next line is in front of you. Lower the presser foot and continue stitching. A cracking corner!

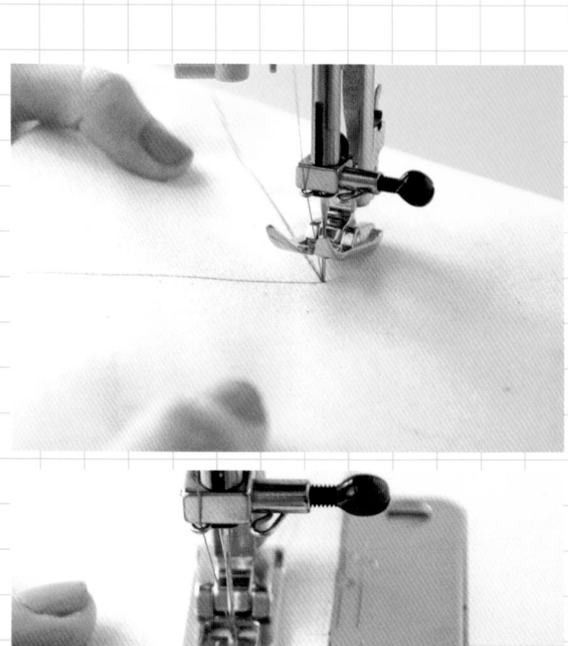

USING THE SEAM ALLOWANCE GUIDE

When you come to sewing pieces of fabric together, you'll be stitching at a certain distance from the raw edge—this distance is known as the seam allowance. The seam allowance that has been added to most home sewing patterns is ⅝" (1.5 cm)—although do check first whenever you use a pattern, as they can vary.

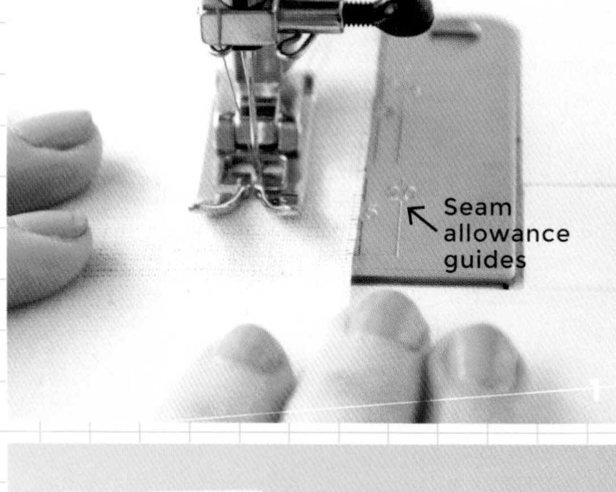

1 See those different line markings and numbers on the throat plate under the presser foot? Those are seam allowance guides, telling you how many fractions of an inch (millimeters) they are away from the needle. Keeping the raw edge of your fabric aligned with one of those guides will allow you to stitch at an even distance from the edge. Practice stitching with a ⅝" (1.5 cm) seam allowance, keeping the raw edge of your fabric lined up with the ⅝" (1.5 cm) guide line.

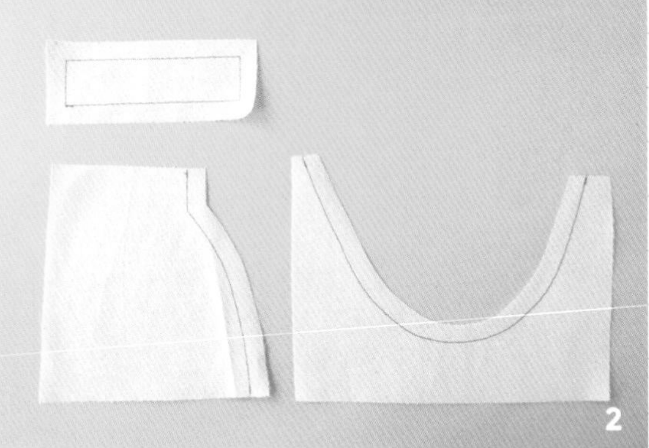

2 Now try cutting some of the shapes shown in the photo—these are some of the shapes you'll come across in the sewing patterns in this book. Then practice using the seam allowance guide to stitch lines ⅝" (1.5 cm) away from the edges. Some involve pivoting corners—it may take a bit of trial, error, and using the handwheel to get to the point of the corner, ⅝" (1.5 cm) from the edge, or you could always mark it in first.

And now you can machine stitch! So let's get cracking and make something already . . .

TO MAKE THE HEAD SCARF

❶ Make a paper pattern piece. Draw a rectangle onto paper, 25½" (65 cm) long by 6" (15 cm) wide, and cut it out with paper scissors (remember, don't use your fabric scissors on paper). Fold your fabric in half widthwise and pin the paper pattern piece to the fabric so that one short edge is lined up with the fold—cutting the fabric on the fold like this will result in a piece double the length of the pattern piece. Avoid pinning the pattern piece to the woven edges of the fabric (the "selvages")—you don't want to use those in your scarf, as they are woven slightly differently than the rest of the fabric.

❷ Cut out the fabric around the paper pattern piece. Cut slowly and evenly around the paper pattern piece, close to the edge of the paper.

❸ Fold the fabric piece in half lengthwise. Position the side that you want showing on the outside of the scarf (the "right side" of the fabric) on the inside of the fold. Press along the foldline. If you want diagonal ends on your scarf, cut them now. Pin together the raw edges. You're going to leave an opening in the stitching so you can turn the scarf right side out later; make two small markings near the middle of the long raw edge, 3–4" (8–10 cm) apart. You can mark with a chalk pencil, washable pen, or a tiny snip into the edge of the fabric.

4 Sew the scarf. Using a ⅝" (1.5 cm) seam allowance, start stitching from one short end, backstitching to secure the stitches. Pivot at the corner, and stitch along the long raw edge until you reach the first marking. Backstitch to secure and trim the threads. Start stitching again from the second marking, backstitching to secure, pivoting again at the corner, stitching down the other short edge, and backstitching to secure the end. Trim the threads.

4

PINNING

TECHNIQUE

Pinning fabric pieces together before stitching helps keep them in place. Here are three great tips for pinning joy.

While it's tempting to use up your whole pin box to keep your fabric from budging, too many pins can distort the fabric and prevent it from lying flat. So try not to go crazy with the pins. Use just enough pins to hold the pieces of fabric together, unless you're stitching something like gathers, in which case, the more the merrier!

There are no rules on which direction to put your pins in—or if there are, I never got the memo. I like to insert mine perpendicular to the edge of the fabric, with the pinhead sticking outward. That way the head doesn't distort the fabric and you can easily whip the pins out when machine stitching.

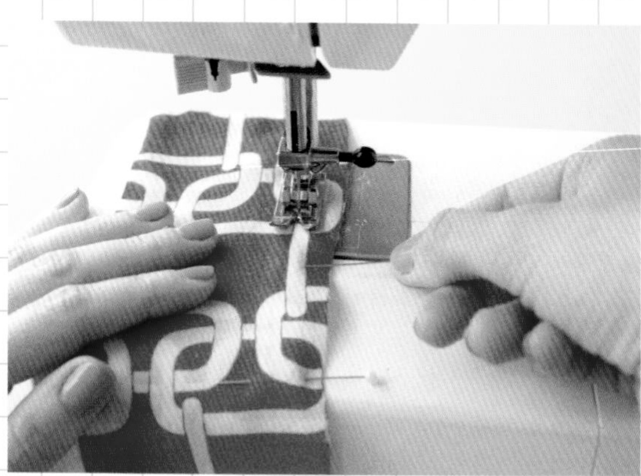

Beware machine stitching over pins! You may think you've gotten away with it, but over time it can damage your machine. Remove each pin just before your presser foot goes over it.

DIFFERENT SCARF SHAPES

You can adjust the shape and size of the scarf to your preference. Try making a cute little neck tie by cutting your paper pattern 16" (40 cm) long by 6" (15 cm) wide.

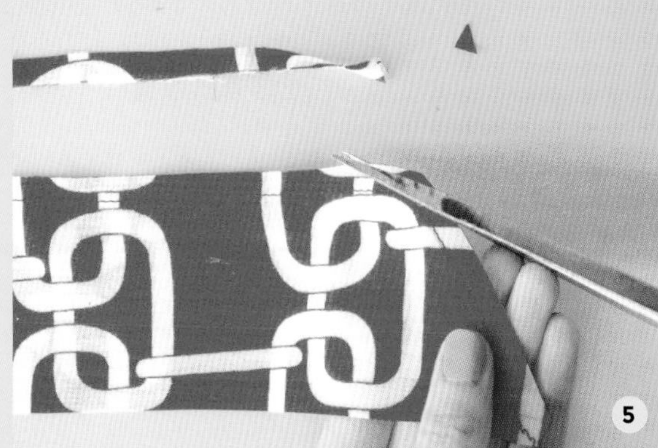

5

❺ **Trim the scarf seam allowances.** Trim them down to about half their original width. Snip diagonally across the corners, about ⅛" (3 mm) from the stitching and being careful not to cut through the stitches. These steps will help make the seams less bulky.

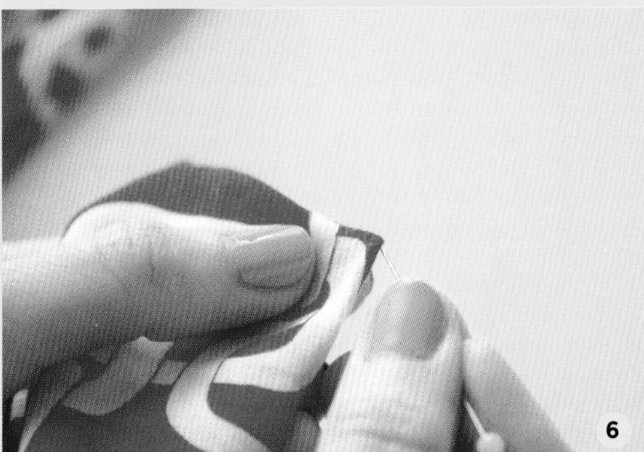

6

❻ **Turn the scarf right side out.** Turn it right side out through the opening in the stitching, then use a pin to gently pull each corner out into a point.

❼ **Press the seams with your iron to neaten them.** At the opening, turn the raw edges to the inside of the scarf and press the folds.

7

❽ **Stitch the opening closed.** Sew a line of stitches close to the edge along the opening to seal it, backstitching at each end.

8

Ooh la la! You made a scarf!

ADJUSTING STITCHES

TECHNIQUE

Now that you've mastered the art of basic machine stitching, play around with the different functions on your machine to see what it's capable of.

The stitch selector knob or buttons allow you to switch between different types of stitches—straight, zigzag, buttonhole, fancy patterns. Test some of the stitches on some scrap fabric.

The stitch length knob or button will set your machine to make longer or shorter stitches. Usually this should be set at about ¹⁄₁₆–⅛" (1.5–3 mm). You'll use long stitches when it comes to machine-basting and gathering, and shorter stitches can be good for navigating curves, for example.

You may need to adjust the thread tension dial to suit a particular fabric or thread. Before starting a project, always test the tension on two scrap layers of the fabric you'll be using. Check that the stitches look even on both sides, and that there aren't any loose loops or tight knots on the surface of the fabric. If there are, try adjusting the tension dial until the stitching looks balanced. Tension is also controlled by the bobbin case, so very occasionally you may need to adjust the screw on the side of the case.

TROUBLESHOOTING CHECKLIST

Occasionally your sewing machine may act up and spit out annoying knots, crazy-looking loops, or petulant puckers. Before you lose your cool, run through this list of common setbacks to see if you can fix the problem.

- Are your spool and bobbin both threaded the right way?
- Is your presser foot down to avoid tensionless stitching chaos?
- Is your needle in the highest position when you start stitching to avoid the machine unthreading itself?
- Are you starting stitching at least ⅛" (3 mm) in from the edge of the fabric so the threads don't get tangled up?
- Is the needle you're using the right size and type for the fabric you're working with?
- Has the bobbin run out of thread?
- Before you start stitching, are both threads sticking out toward the back so they don't tie themselves into a mess?

Hopefully you've managed to diagnose and solve the problem with this troubleshooting checklist. If not, there's always the Internet!

WHY

I MADE IT MYSELF!

MAKE IT YOUR OWN

Scarves are super-easy and quick to sew, don't take lots of fabric, and are a major asset to every dressmaker's wardrobe.

SQUARE NECK SCARF

If your style is less Brigitte Bardot and more Faye Dunaway in *Bonnie and Clyde*, try making a simple square neck scarf. This variation will introduce you to hemming raw edges, which will come up a lot in dressmaking.

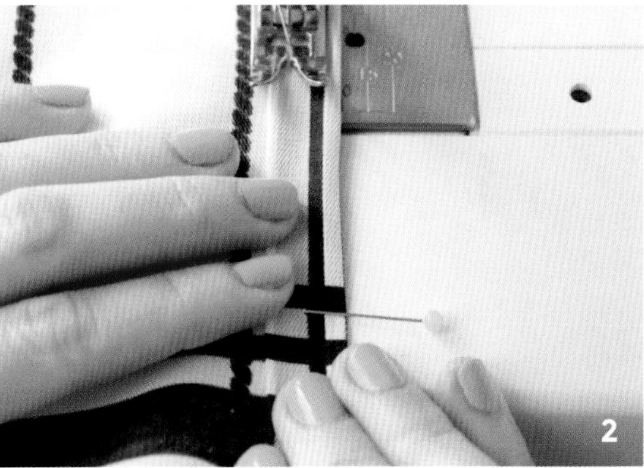

2

1 Draw a square onto paper, about 24" x 24" (60 cm x 60 cm) for a small scarf or 32" x 32" (80 cm x 80 cm) for a large one. Cut out the paper pattern piece and pin it to your fabric, keeping one side parallel to (but not exactly on) the woven selvage edges of the fabric. Cut out your fabric around the paper pattern.

Turn each of the four raw edges under by ⅝" (1.5 cm) and press with your iron. Turn the folded edges under by another ⅝" (1.5 cm) and press again. Pin the folds to hold them in place.

2 Stitch the folds down, using the ⅜" (1 cm) seam allowance guide and pivoting at each corner. Rather than backstitching, since you're sewing full circle (or, technically, full square), you can finish by sewing a few stitches directly on top of the first stitches to secure them.

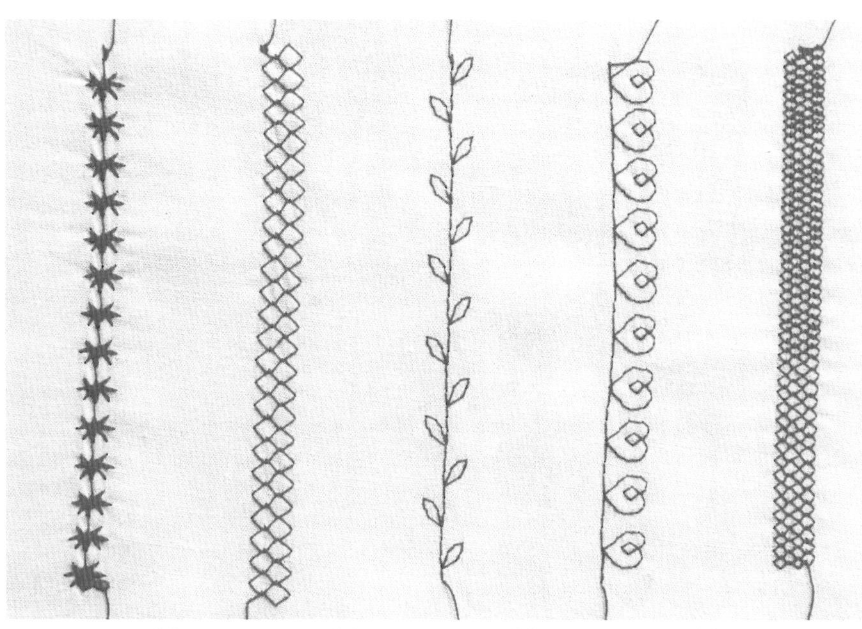

EMBELLISH WITH TOPSTITCHING

These days even the most basic sewing machine usually comes with a number of fancy stitch settings. While some of these stitches are functional, many are purely decorative—from geometric patterns to flowers. Try adding a pretty stitch design to the edge of your scarf for an extra-special touch.

Use a contrasting thread so your stitching shows up against the fabric. Regular thread will work fine for topstitching lightweight to medium-weight fabrics, or you could try special topstitching thread, which is thicker and more noticeable—use it on the spool only, with regular thread in the bobbin.

Test your stitches on a doubled scrap of fabric before you begin, adjusting the thread tension if necessary until the stitches lay nicely without bunching up the fabric. Steam pressing before and after stitching will help keep the stitches nice and smooth.

When you're ready to sew, try to keep the line of stitching at an equal distance from the edge of the fabric, stitching as slowly as you need to and using the seam allowance guide to help you. Begin and end the decorative topstitching by backstitching with a straight stitch to secure it.

Now that you've mastered the art of decorative topstitching, try adding it to other projects, such as the hem of the Clémence Skirt (pages 116–37) or the neckline on the Lilou Dress (pages 162–77).

MAKE IT A LIFESTYLE

FEARLESS SEWING

Embarking on a new endeavor such as sewing is exciting and fulfilling yet can sometimes cause a little anxiety at the same time. Learning to operate a sewing machine or tackling a buttonhole can take you outside of your comfort zone and into the territory of the unknown. It's a potentially risky strategy—what if you mess it up and feel incompetent? Yet think back to what you were like as a kid tackling anything new—whether it was tearing open the box of a toy to see how it worked, diving into a chemistry experiment at school, or making up your own recipes at home. No fear, just a willingness to experiment and a joy in discovery. How about channeling your childlike self and reigniting that sense of play in your dressmaking?

Sometimes it's the fear of ruining special fabric that holds us back from plunging into a project. If you find this is the case, consider lowering your quality threshold and using fabric that you are happy to cut into without worry. If you're tackling something tricky, such as inserting a gathered sleeve, you can always machine-baste first as a practice run, using longer stitches in a contrasting thread. Once you're happy with your stitching, sew the seams for real and remove the basting. As your confidence builds, you'll probably find you baste less and less.

Most mistakes can be corrected with a seam ripper. Keeping this nifty little tool close at hand can act as a comfort blanket, removing the fear factor, as you know it's there if you need it. Slip the blade under stitches that need correcting (every fourth stitch or so in a seam should do it) and pull them out. Then sew that part again, overlapping the new stitches over the ends of the existing stitches to secure them.

Try not to go overboard with the seam ripper though, or you may just be sitting at your sewing table forever. When you buy a dress in a store, or admire one that someone else is wearing, chances are you don't notice things like a few wrinkles in the fabric, mismatched stripes, or even the odd wonky stitch. But when you make a garment yourself, you're staring at these details close up for hours, so it's inevitable that they become so much more obvious. If you're stressing out over something like that, try leaving it for a bit and come back to it later. It'll probably seem much less of an issue after a break from staring at it for so long.

Mistakes will happen. Even the most experienced dressmaker messes things up occasionally. And, as the old adage goes, that's how we learn. So dive in fearlessly, and don't be so hard on yourself if things don't turn out perfectly. Sewing means a lot to me, and I love to create beautiful things, but it is only sewing—a dodgy seam isn't going to ruin my or anyone else's life. So let's remember we're doing this for fun, let's take pleasure in the process, and let's be proud of our finished makes, the odd wonky stitch and all.

MARGOT PAJAMAS

CHAPTER 2

We've sewn something flat, now it's time to get three-dimensional! The Margot pajama pants make a perfect first garment project. Easy to sew, easy to fit, no tricky fastenings, plus you don't have to wear them out of the house so there's no need to stress if the stitching is a bit wonky! Make a lightweight pair for summer and a snuggly pair for winter, then you can wear handmade in bed all year round.

SUPPLIES

2½ yd (2.3 m) length of fabric, 60" (150 cm) wide

OR 2¾ yd (2.5 m) length of fabric, 45" (115 cm) wide

Thread (in color to match your fabric)

TOOLS

See page 14

OPTIONAL

⅜" (1 cm) wide ribbon, instead of drawstring, the length of half of your waist measurement plus 20" (50 cm)

TECHNIQUES

Setting up your sewing machine (page 21)

Stitching school (page 26)

Pinning (page 30)

Adjusting stitches (page 32)

Choosing your fabric (page 44)

Preparing your pattern (page 47)

Laying out fabric and pattern (page 48)

Cutting out fabric pieces (page 50)

Transferring the markings (page 52)

Understanding clothing construction (page 54)

Simple seam allowance finishes (page 55)

Pressing matters (page 57)

Hemming (page 60)

FABRIC SUGGESTIONS

Choose a soft lightweight to medium-weight cotton, such as lawn, shirting, double gauze, or quilting cotton. Flannel will make a cozy option for the colder months. If you're a confident stitcher, how about creating some silk pj's for the boudoir?

PATTERN DETAILS

The paper pattern has 2 pieces:

Front leg—cut 2

Back leg—cut 2

If you want to make a drawstring in matching fabric, cut two long strips of fabric, each 1½" (4 cm) wide by the length of half of your waist measurement plus 10" (25 cm). Alternatively, you could use ⅜" (1 cm) wide ribbon.

Seam allowance is ⅝" (1.5 cm).

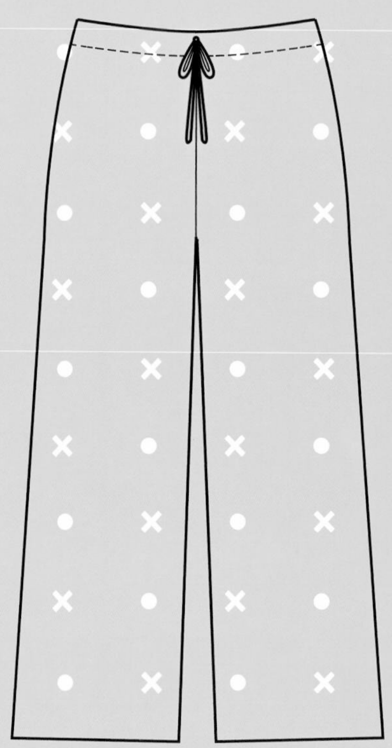

PATTERN SIZING

BODY MEASUREMENTS

SIZE	WAIST	HIP
1	24" (61 cm)	33" (84 cm)
2	26" (66 cm)	35" (89 cm)
3	28" (71 cm)	37" (94 cm)
4	30" (76 cm)	39" (99 cm)
5	32" (81 cm)	41" (104 cm)
6	34" (86.5 cm)	43" (109 cm)
7	36" (91.5 cm)	45" (114 cm)
8	38" (96.5 cm)	47" (119.5 cm)

FINISHED GARMENT MEASUREMENTS

SIZE	HIP
1	37½" (95 cm)
2	39½" (100 cm)
3	41½" (105 cm)
4	43½" (110.5 cm)
5	45½" (115.5 cm)
6	47½" (120.5 cm)
7	49½" (125.5 cm)
8	51½" (131 cm)

Note: Waist is adjustable using drawstring.

FABRIC LAYOUT

Here is the suggested arrangement of the pattern pieces on the fabric.

60" (150 cm) wide fabric

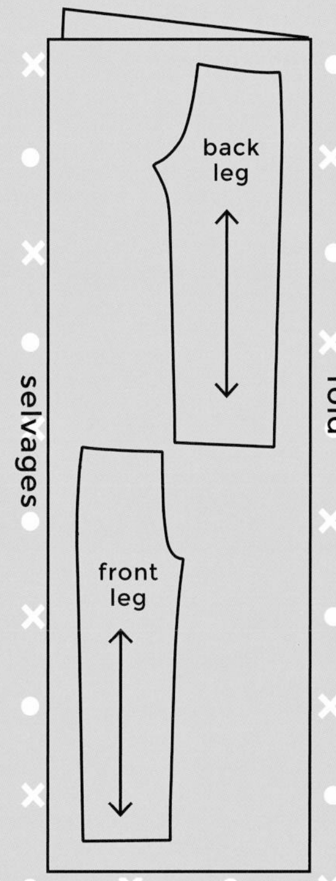

45" (115 cm) wide fabric

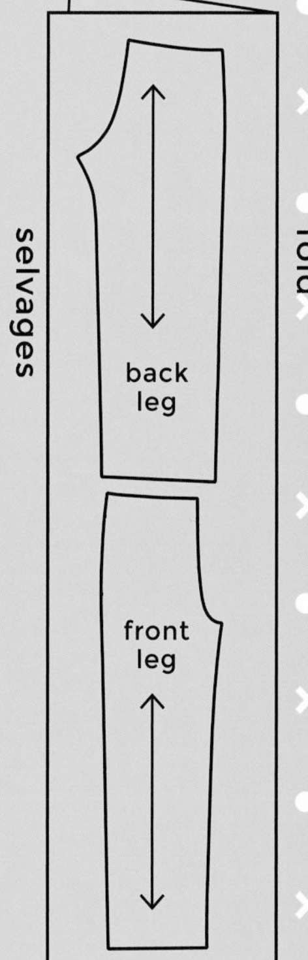

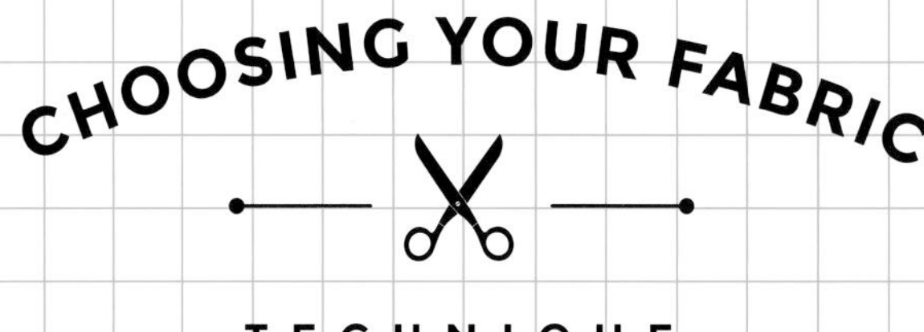

TECHNIQUE

The fabric you choose can play a major role in determining whether your dressmaking project becomes a wardrobe favorite or destined for the trash. When I first began sewing, I made a few bad fabric decisions, most memorably the blouse that felt like a suit of armor and thus sadly never saw the outside world. Each project in this book includes a list of suggested fabrics that are easy to find, easy to handle, and will work well with the particular garment to help you avoid making a similar mistake.

As your experience grows, you'll be able to go "off list" and choose other types of fabric with similar properties. It's definitely worth doing a little homework to build up your fabric-choosing prowess. Spend some time in a fabric store touching all the different fabrics—get a feel for their texture, thickness, and how they hang. If you can, build up a small collection of swatches and attach them to a labeled list so you have a reference guide for later. But you don't need to be a fabric expert to be a successful home dressmaker. In fact, in this book I'm deliberately not overwhelming you with too many obscure fabric names, or expecting you to know the difference between mousseline and crêpe de chine, as it can become really confusing. Just find the fabrics that work for you.

Here are a few considerations to help you choose fabric for your project.

HOW EASY WILL IT BE TO SEW?

Without a doubt certain fabrics are easier to handle than others—those others, they'll slip away from your cutting tools, have a party with your needle, slip off the table into the wastepaper basket while your head is turned. If you're a beginner, there are certain fabrics I'd advise you to avoid like the plague. I'm looking at you, silk chiffon. Save them until you're more confident on the machine. Or never sew them ever if you don't want to—I'm not judging. The fabrics suggested for the patterns in this book are much easier to work with. My personal favorites include cotton voile for floaty blouses, gabardine or drill for a shaped skirt, double gauze for snuggly pajamas, and interlock knit or double knit for a comfy dress.

DRAPEY OR STIFF?

The trap I fell into when I began sewing, and which I see happening to others all the time, is to pick a fabric with too much or too little drape for the garment in question. What was designed to be an elegant sleeve in a drapey lawn or silk can end up an awkward puff if made in stiff quilting cotton. Equally, a structured skirt such as Delphine (page 68) will lose its defined shape if made in a drapey material. Hold up some fabric and see how it hangs—will it produce a flowing shape suitable for a chic blouse or dress, or does it hold its shape nicely for a structured skirt or jacket?

HEAVY OR LIGHT?

The thickness and weight of a fabric will impact the finished look and feel of the garment. For example, the same button-front bodice pattern could produce totally different results depending on how heavy the fabric is: a blouse if made in lightweight cotton or more of a jacket if made in heavyweight wool.

WOVEN OR STRETCH?

The projects in this book are all designed for woven fabrics. Jersey or knit fabrics with stretch

behave differently than woven fabrics, so patterns suitable for them will have been drafted to account for their stretch. An exception is interlock knit or double knit, which is more stable than regular knits, and can be used instead of woven fabrics on some projects, such as the Megan Dress (page 92). If you decide to make Megan in double knit, use a ballpoint or stretch needle in your sewing machine.

PRINT OR SOLID COLOR?

In my first ever sewing lesson, I always remember the teacher advising us to choose a busy print for our dresses as it hides dodgy stitching! This is a great tip, but try not to get caught up in the snazzy print trap for all of your sewing life. Solid colors can look really striking and can show off details in the garment design that admirers of your handmade wardrobe might otherwise miss. Another tip is to avoid stripes when you're just starting out, as matching them up at the seams can be a pain. Unless you're not bothered by wonky or mismatched stripes, in which case, I salute you—life's too short, my friend!

IS IT MACHINE WASHABLE?

I don't know about you, but I loathe both hand washing and going to the dry cleaners. Don't tell anyone, but my beautiful red mohair sweater has been sulking at the bottom of the laundry basket for about three years now (sssshhh!). So I always look for machine-washable fabrics to sew with and ask about the laundry requirements before buying if I'm unsure. Throw garments in the washing machine and you leave yourself more time to sew—hooray!

For more tips on fabric shopping, turn to page 64.

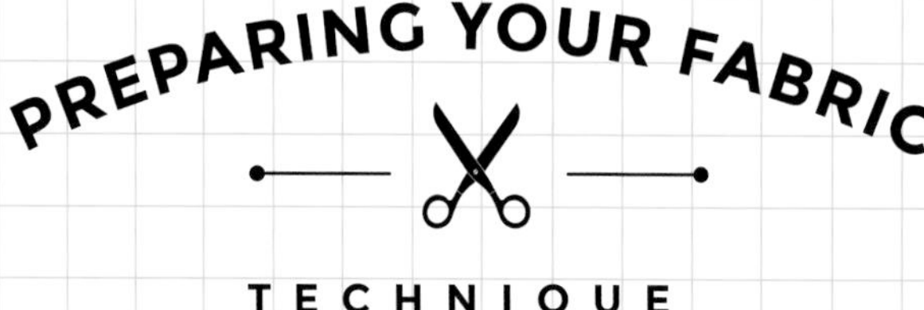

PREPARING YOUR FABRIC

TECHNIQUE

Once you've got your hands on your fabric, there are just a couple of things to do before you start sewing it.

WASH IT

I know it sounds boring when all you want to do is start cutting into that fabric, but prewashing your fabric can save you a lot of heartache further down the line. The fabric may shrink a little the first time you wash it, or change the way it hangs or feels, so best get that over with now before you cut out your size and sew it together.

PRESS IT

If your fabric has any creases or wrinkles in it, which is likely after washing, give it a good press with the iron. Smoothing out your fabric will make for much more accurate shapes when you cut it out. Test a small patch first to check that the heat and steam setting on your iron is right for your fabric.

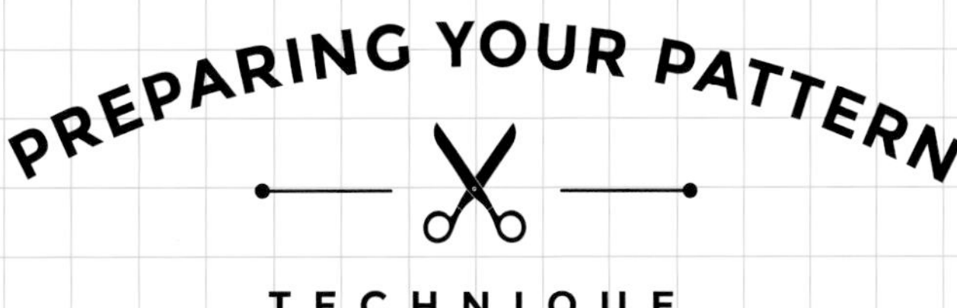

PREPARING YOUR PATTERN

TECHNIQUE

The project patterns are in full-scale, multisized, printed format. Here's how to get them ready to use.

Identify your size on the Body Measurements chart in each chapter. We'll look at measuring and fitting in more detail later in the book, but for the Margot Pajamas you measure whichever is larger of your waist and hips and find the pattern size that corresponds with that measurement.

On the pattern sheets, find the right pattern pieces—the Pattern Details section will tell you what to look for; some of the pieces will be overlapping. When you've identified the pieces, locate the lines corresponding to your size—they are numbered, and there is also a Pattern Size Key that tells you which style of dashed line is your size. You may find it easier to see your size clearly if you highlight these lines with a colored pen.

Trace any overlapping pieces onto a new sheet of paper. You could use flipchart paper, banner paper, or even baking paper taped together: slightly transparent paper is easy to trace through. Alternatively, lay the pattern on top of the paper, roll a tracing wheel over the lines, then go over the traced lines in pencil or pen. As well as tracing the outlines of the pieces, add in grainline arrows, instructional text, and any other markings for your size. Each size usually has its own markings—the innermost markings go with size 1, the next with size 2, and so on. Roughly cut around the pattern pieces, about 1" (2.5 cm) from the outlines.

Store the pattern pieces in a plastic envelope or in the pouch in this book to keep them safe.

TO MAKE THE PAJAMAS

1 Lay out your fabric and place the paper pattern pieces on it.
(See the Laying Out Fabric and Pattern technique, page 48.)

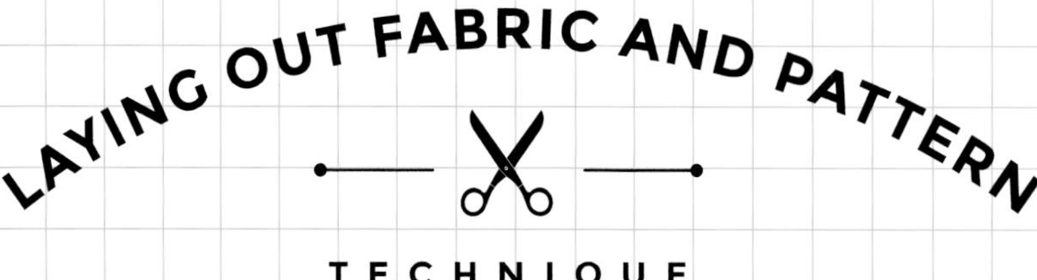

LAYING OUT FABRIC AND PATTERN

TECHNIQUE

Right, let's get our fabric ready to cut. Clear as big a space as you can on a table—and wipe it clean while you're at it.

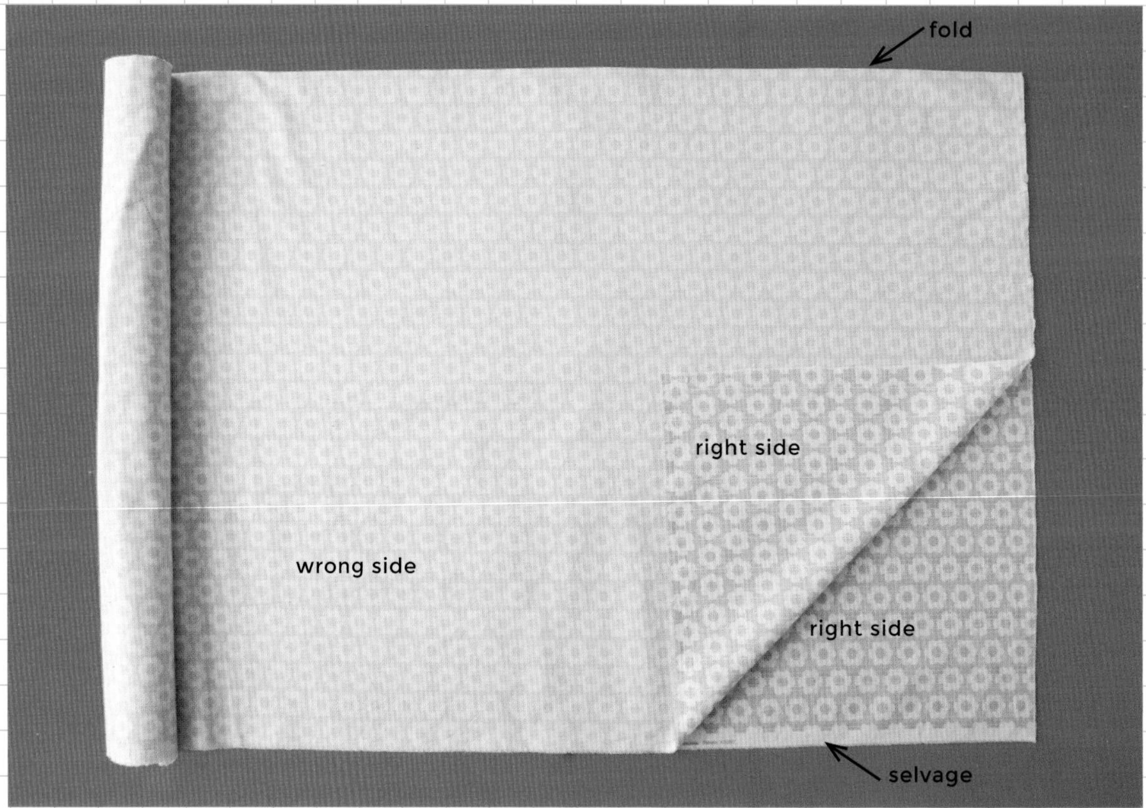

LAYING OUT THE FABRIC

Your fabric has a "right side" and a "wrong side"—the right side will show on the outside of your garment, the wrong side on the inside. If it doesn't have a print on it, there may be a difference in how the weave looks on either side—look closely if it's not immediately obvious which side is which. The woven edges running down either side of the length of the fabric are the selvages.

Fold your fabric in half lengthwise, right sides together, matching up the selvages. Folding it in half allows you to cut two pieces from the same pattern piece at once—or one symmetrical piece for those that say "place on fold." Smooth the fabric out to ensure the selvages are parallel to each other and both sides of fabric are as flat as possible. Unless you have a banquet table in your kitchen or dining room, it's likely that your fabric is going to be too long—that's not a problem; just lay out as much as you can and roll the other end up until you need it.

LAYING OUT THE PATTERN

Now lay out the paper pattern pieces on the fabric. Follow the Fabric Layout provided, or you can play around to see what works with the piece of fabric that you have. The pattern pieces will give you some instructions on positioning. Pin them in place as you go, using enough pins to hold the pattern pieces down but not so many that the pattern is distorted. Alternatively, you can use heavy food cans to hold your pattern in place.

From Chapter 3 onward, some of the patterns include a hooked arrow that says "place on fold." Lay these pieces out first, lining up the indicated edge with the fold of the fabric. (The "place on fold" arrows are not to be confused with the "foldline" on the Margot pattern, which is a sewing instruction that we'll come to later.) By cutting on the fold you'll end up with one symmetrical piece of fabric double the size of the pattern piece.

Next, position any other large pieces, followed by any smaller ones. The double-pointed arrow on each pattern piece indicates the grainline—it's telling you which direction to position the pattern piece in relation to your fabric, and will impact upon the way your garment hangs. Line up the grainline arrow so it runs exactly lengthwise down the fabric, parallel to the selvages. You can use the selvages to help you here—stick a pin in one end of the arrow, measure the distance from one selvage, then pivot the other end of the arrow until it's at the same distance from the selvage, and pin in place.

Both the Pattern Details section and the pattern pieces themselves will tell you to "Cut 1," "Cut 2," etc. Remember that with a double layer of fabric you'll be cutting one piece if the pattern is placed on the fold, or two pieces if it's not.

Where a piece says "Cut 2 + 1 interfacing," this means you need to cut two pieces of fabric and one piece of interfacing.

Sometimes you may find it more economical to fold the fabric into thirds rather than half—if you do this, just make sure the selvages remain parallel to each other.

Avoid pinning fabric onto the selvages themselves—these pieces can be discarded.

Also be aware of any directional prints: if your fabric has trees on it, make sure those trees will end up the right way up on the finished garment!

2 Cut out all the pajama fabric pieces. (See the Cutting Out Fabric Pieces technique, below.)

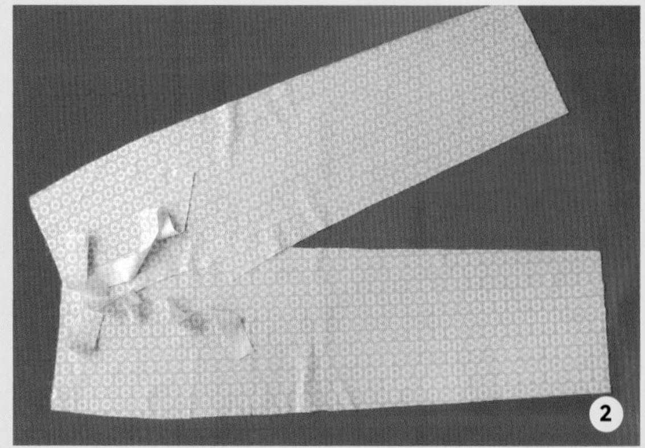

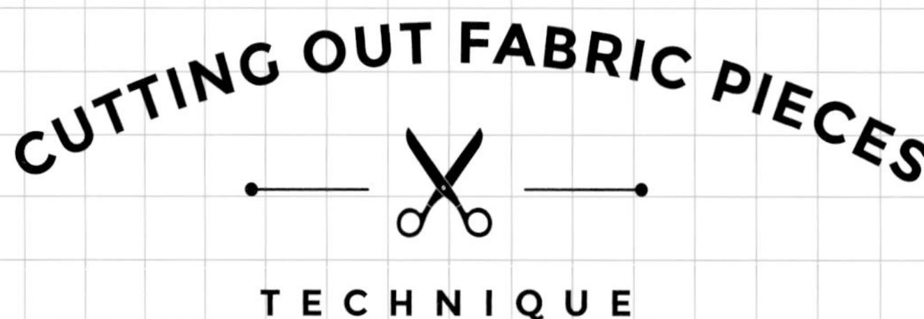

There's more than one way of cutting fabric, so go with the one that works for you.

THE CLASSIC METHOD

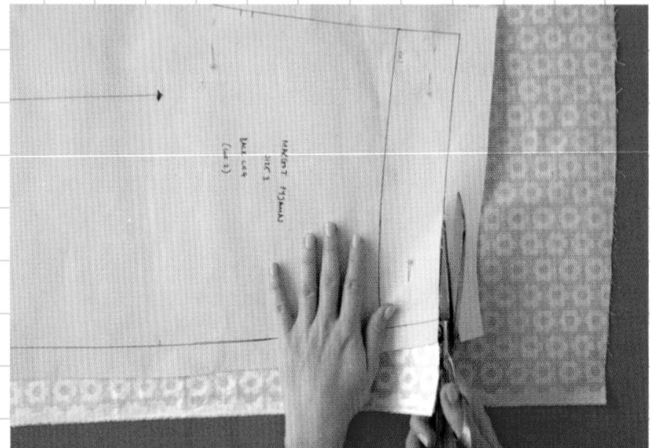

I'm calling this the classic method as it's arguably the most common approach used by DIY dressmakers. Roughly cut around the paper pattern pieces with paper scissors, leaving extra space around the outlines. Pin these pattern pieces to the fabric. Using dressmaking scissors, cut through both paper and fabric, exactly on the pattern piece outlines. This is a simple way to approach cutting, although cutting paper with your dressmaking scissors can dull them over time, plus you'll need to trace off a new copy of the paper pattern each time you make it.

THE OUTLINE METHOD

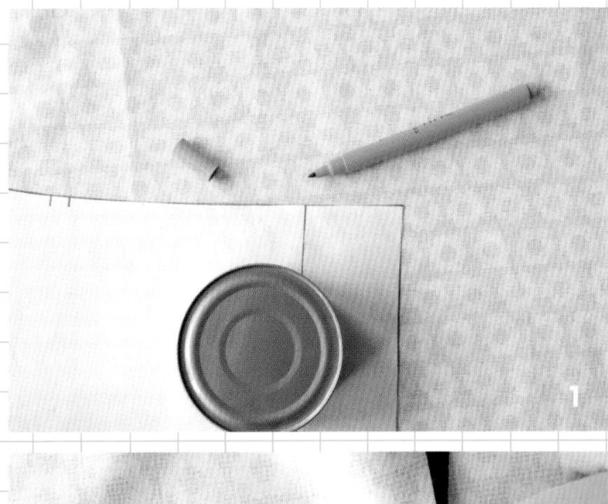

1 Start by cutting out the paper pattern pieces with paper scissors exactly on the outlines. Position the pattern pieces on the fabric, using weights to hold them in place instead of pins. You don't need special weights—food cans or similar will work just fine. Using sharp chalk or a washable pen, draw exactly around the outline of each pattern piece, keeping your chalk or pen pressed up against the edge of the paper.

2 Remove the paper pattern and cut the fabric just within the drawn lines. You can use either dressmaking scissors or a rotary cutter, which is a sharp rolling blade on a handle. When working with a rotary cutter, use a cutting mat to protect your table and be really careful of your fingers! This method usually results in more accurate cutting than the classic method, as the fabric stays flatter on the table.

THE TRACING METHOD

. . . Also known as Tilly's Favorite Method: I urge you to try this!

Roughly cut around the paper pattern pieces with paper scissors, leaving extra space around the outlines. Position these pattern pieces on the fabric, and hold them in place using either weights or pins. Slip a sheet of dressmaker's carbon underneath the edge of the pattern, face down against the fabric. With a cutting mat underneath the fabric, run a tracing wheel directly on top of the lines to transfer them to your fabric. Move the dressmaker's carbon around as you need to, and mark in darts the same way.

Remove the pattern and cut the fabric exactly along the outlines, using dressmaking scissors or a rotary cutter. The beauty of this method is not only that it's accurate but you can also reuse the pattern many times without having to trace it first.

Whichever way you choose to cut your fabric, try to keep it as flat as possible against the table—you can use the hand you're not cutting with to gently hold the pattern and fabric in place.

Unless you're cutting short or curved lines, make long cuts with the full length of the scissor blades—not little snips with the tips—to keep the lines nice and even.

Take your time to cut as accurately as you can so you don't end up with a garment that's too big or too small for you.

3 Transfer the pajama pattern markings. Carefully and accurately transfer all the markings onto the cut-out fabric pieces (see the Transferring the Markings technique, below).

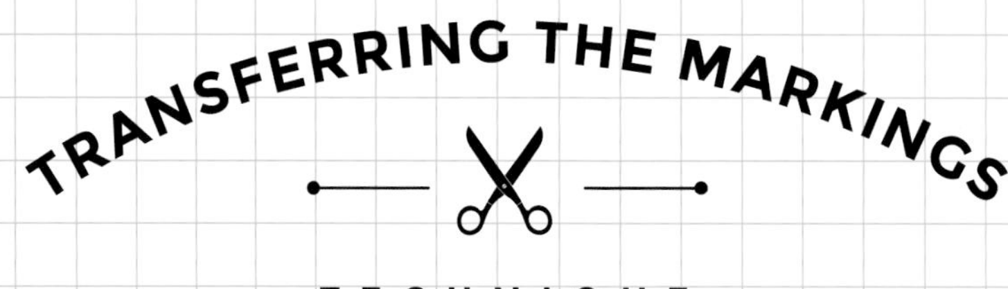

TRANSFERRING THE MARKINGS TECHNIQUE

Your paper pattern pieces have all sorts of information written all over them, some of which you need to transfer to the fabric before you remove the pattern. Don't worry about transferring the text labeling or the grainlines, but do mark the following:

NOTCHES

The small lines perpendicular to the cutting lines indicate notches. Marking notches will help you match the pieces accurately when you pin them together. Two notches next to each other signify the back of a pattern piece. Mark each notch with a small snip shorter than the seam allowance. (Other sewing patterns often indicate notches with a small triangle.)

SMALL CIRCLES OR CROSSES

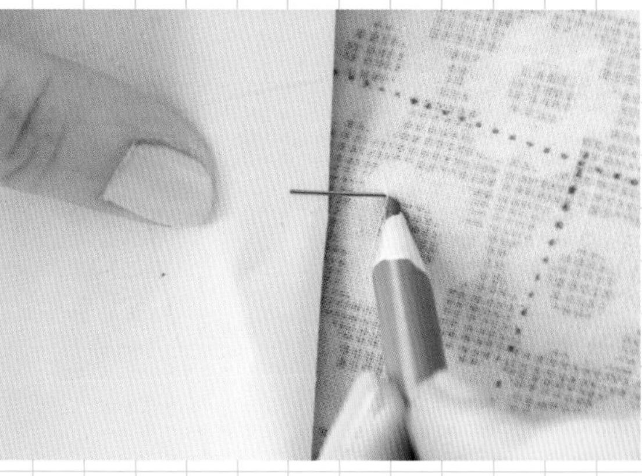

Small circles or crosses usually show you where to start or stop a line of stitching. For example, the pair of circles near the front crotch seam of the Margot Pajamas mark the gap that should be left for the drawstring opening, and the circles on the Megan and Mimi sleeve caps (pages 105 and 146) show the start and end points of the gathering stitches for ease. Stick a pin through the center of the circles through all layers of pattern and fabric. Pull the pieces apart slightly and mark the penetration point (behave!) of the pin with a chalk pencil or washable pen.

DARTS, PLEATS, AND OTHER LINES

Other lines on the pattern could include darts (shown as a large triangle—page 100), pleats (page 170), foldlines (such as those on the Margot Pajamas), or buttonholes. I like to mark them using dressmaker's carbon and a tracing wheel, in the same way I mark the pattern pieces. Alternatively, you could mark the points with a washable pen as outlined above, then draw between the lines.

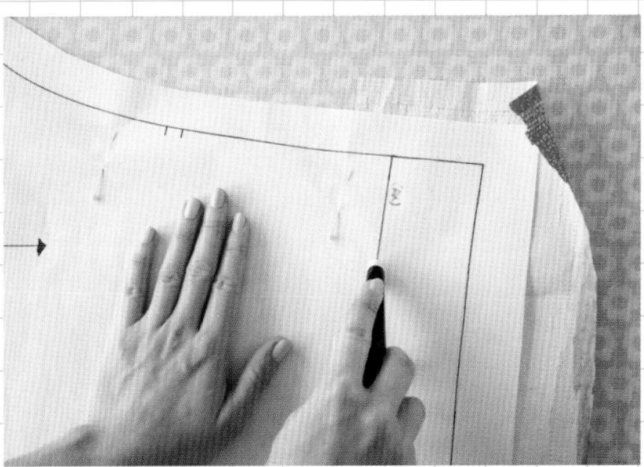

❹ **Pin the fabric leg pieces together to make two complete pajama legs.** Place one front leg against one back leg, right sides together, matching notches, and pin together the inside and outside legs (the front legs are the ones with a single notch at the crotch, the back legs have double notches). Do the same with the other leg (see the Understanding Clothing Construction technique, page 54).

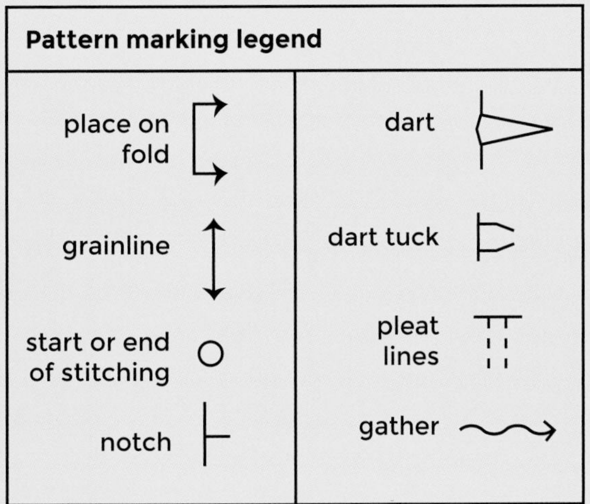

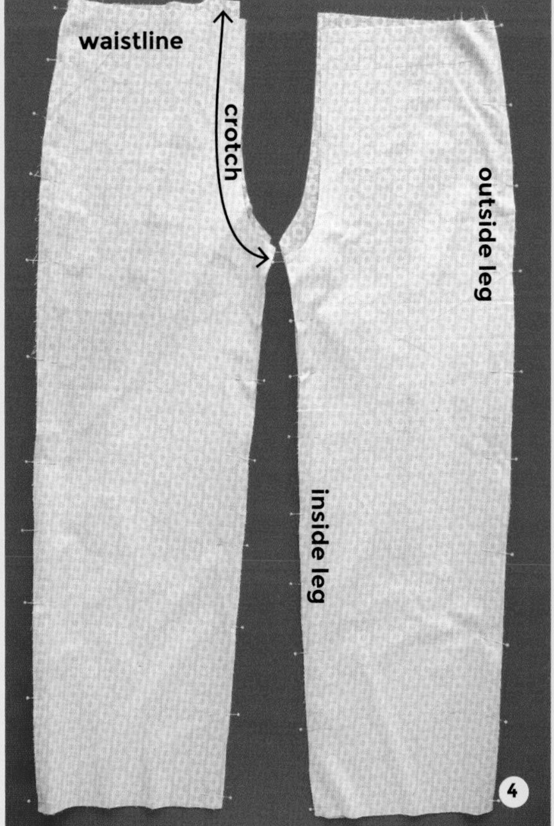

UNDERSTANDING CLOTHING CONSTRUCTION

TECHNIQUE

The first few times you put pieces of fabric together can seem like a whole new—and confusing—world, but it'll soon make sense. Take a peek inside existing clothing to get a feel for garment construction; start by having a look at a pair of pajama pants to see which edges are joined. The patterns in this book have some parts and seams labeled so you can quickly see what is what.

When pinning pieces of fabric together, the right sides (the sides that will be on the outside) will usually be touching each other. This way the stitching and seam allowances will end up hidden on the inside of the garment. Line up the raw edges with each other, matching the notches that you've snipped to help align them accurately.

Not all seams will look like they are going to match up as the pieces are often different shapes. However, the seamlines as sewn together will be the same length (unless there is ease or gathering, which we'll come to later). Just make sure you're pinning the raw edges together, even if that means bending the fabric a little, rather than laying the pieces flat on top of each other.

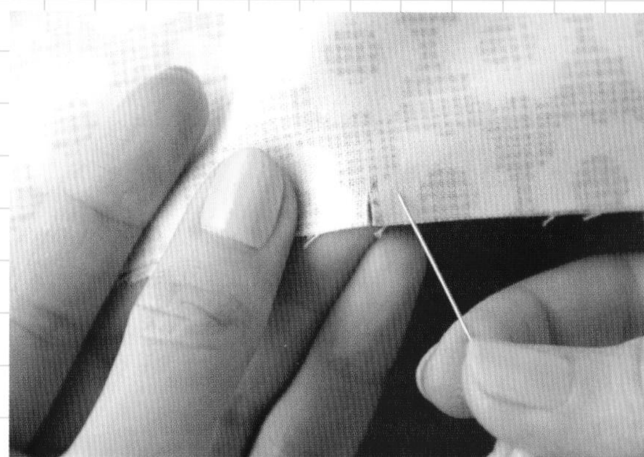

5 Stitch the pajama leg seams. Stitch the inside leg seams (not the crotch) and the outside leg seams as pinned, using a $\frac{5}{8}$" (1.5 cm) seam allowance and backstitching at each end. Do the same with the other leg.

5

6 Trim the seam allowances. Cut the $\frac{5}{8}$" (1.5 cm) seam allowances to about half their width. Finish each seam allowance using zigzag stitch or an overlocker (see the Simple Seam Allowance Finishes technique, page 55).

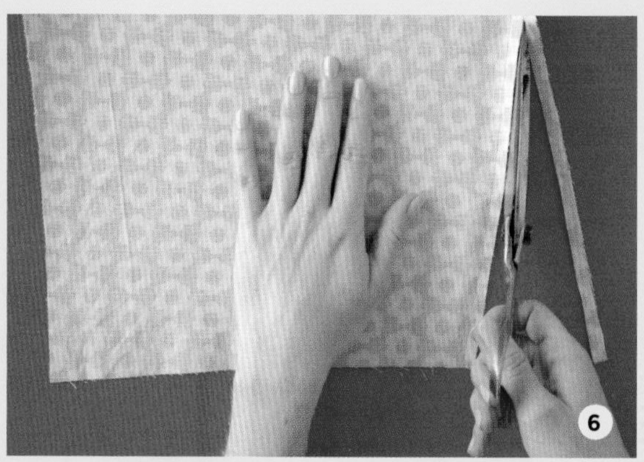

6

SIMPLE SEAM ALLOWANCE FINISHES

TECHNIQUE

"Finishing" seam allowances means tidying them up so the raw edges won't fray. There are different ways of doing this, some more suited to particular fabrics than others, but you don't need to learn them all yet. Zigzag stitch and the overlocker are covered here, and then you'll be taken up a level on page 123 with French seams. Finish seam allowances as you go, before you stitch a new line across them.

ZIGZAG FINISHING

Zigzag stitching is a simple way of tidying up the seam allowances of your garment. You can zigzag stitch the two seam allowances together if you're sewing a side seam and the fabric is fairly lightweight, or zigzag each seam allowance separately. Start by trimming the seam allowances down, but not too narrow: about half their width is fine.

1 Set your machine to the zigzag stitch setting. It's a good idea to test the position, stitch length, and tension of the zigzag on a scrap of fabric first and adjust if necessary. You want the right side of the zigzag to land just at the edge of the fabric, and the left side of the zigzag to fall within the seam allowance. Don't backstitch the ends—instead, tie the threads into a double knot by hand. Press the seam allowances either open or together toward the back of the garment.

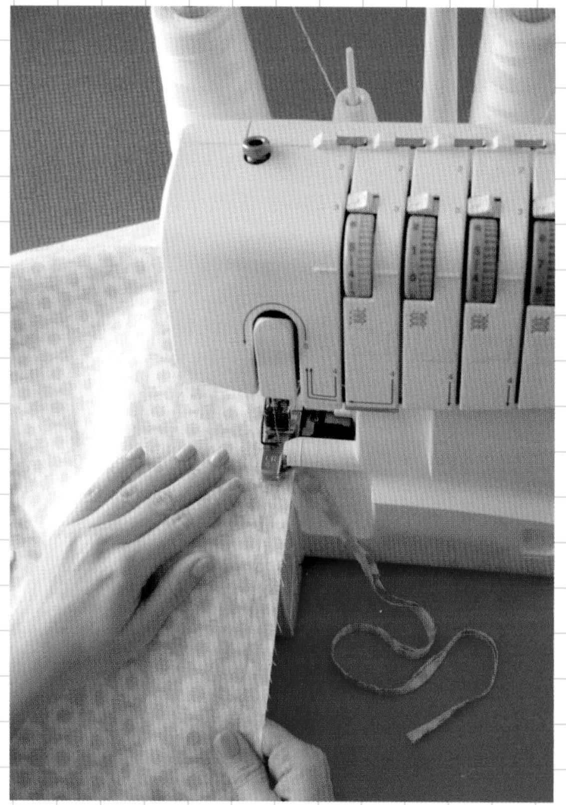

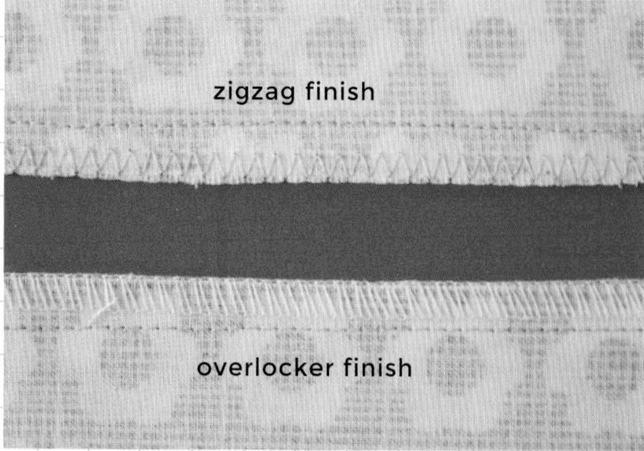

GETTING AN OVERLOCKER

An overlocker (a serger) is a separate machine that's really useful for creating a professional-looking finish on your seam allowances. It wraps multiple threads around the raw edges of the fabric, and also trims the seam allowances as part of the process. An overlocker is certainly not essential when you're just starting sewing, but if you—hopefully—get really into it and want to invest in a great piece of equipment, I heartily recommend an overlocker to make your garments look awesome. It's also useful for sewing stretch fabrics.

❼ **Press all of the pajama leg seam allowances.** Press them either open or together toward the back (see the Pressing Matters technique, opposite).

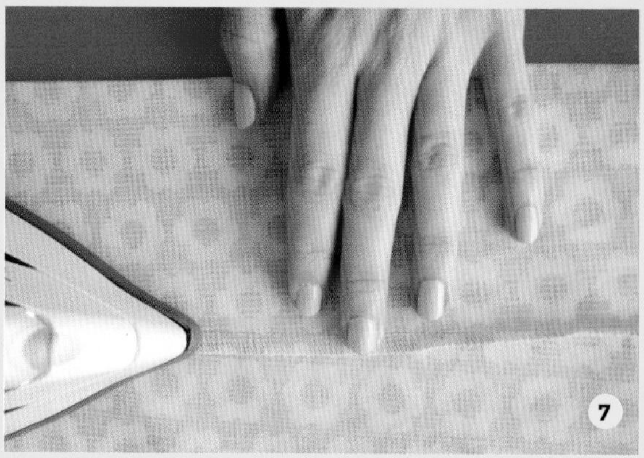

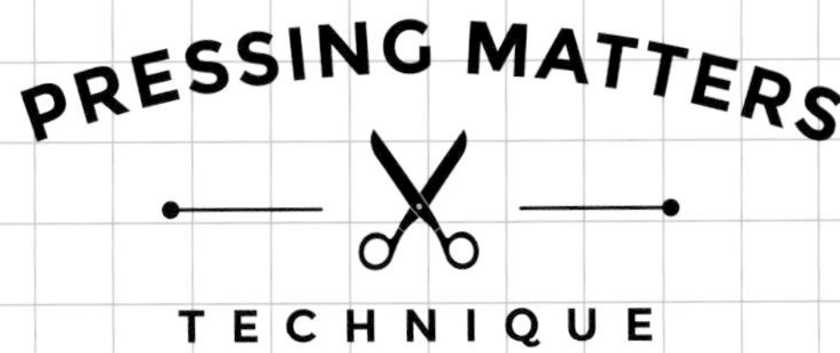

TECHNIQUE

PRESSING MATTERS

Thought pressing was boring? Think again, my friend! Before I began sewing, I admit the ironing board rarely saw the light of day in my apartment, but all that changed when I started creating my own clothes. The iron became my friend and ally. Pressing can make any sewing project look miles better by flattening seams, adding definition to stitching lines, shaping darts elegantly, and generally making everything look much neater.

So what's the difference between pressing and ironing, you ask? When pressing, you're placing the iron onto the fabric, holding it static for a few seconds, then lifting it up and placing it on another part of the fabric. Ironing, however, involves a back-and-forth movement to smooth out creases. Now you can impress your friends with your worldly knowledge!

TIPS AND TRICKS FOR PRESSING JOY

- You don't have to get up after stitching every seam and go over to the ironing board; you can "save up" bits that need pressing and do them in one go, as long as the iron gets to them before you stitch again across that area.
- Different fabrics can tolerate different amounts of heat and steam—too high and they may become marked or could even melt. So test the iron on a small swatch first before attacking the whole thing. You can help avoid damaging your fabric by laying a pressing cloth over it to protect it from the direct heat of the iron. A piece of muslin, cotton, or even a clean dishtowel will do just fine.
- Press on both the wrong and right sides of the fabric to get a neat finish.
- Seam allowances can either be pressed open or toward the back of the garment. It's a good idea to press them flat first, as they were stitched, to "set" the stitching into the fabric.
- Don't be afraid of a bit of steam. As long as your fabric can take it, steam will soften your fabric and help you mold and manipulate it into the shape you want it to be. For instance, it can help you roll a facing to the inside of the garment, or it can make a pointy bust dart look a little more curved and a lot less rude.
- Avoid pressing gathers; it's too easy to ruin the lovely fullness you've created with your stitching.
- Use just the tip of your iron to press seams where you don't want to flatten the surrounding fabric. You can also position the seam along the edge of your ironing board and let the fabric hang off the side so it doesn't touch the iron.
- If you're really fancy, you can get a tailor's ham and seam roll. These are specially shaped, dedicated pressing devices that look like pillows but are deceptively firm. A tailor's ham will help you press curved parts of a garment such as darts or collars; a seam roll is a cylindrical shape that lets you press just the middle of a seam without creating a ridge on the seam edges. Or you could get creative with a makeshift alternative—roll up a towel tightly into the shape you need for the part of the garment you're pressing. That's what I do!
- At the risk of sounding like your mother, don't forget to turn the iron off when you're not using it! Not only will conserving the energy save the planet (or something like that), but if you knock it over and burn yourself you'll have to stop sewing for the day, and that would be annoying.

8 Join the two pajama legs together at the crotch seam. The easiest way to get the two legs' right sides together along the length of the crotch seam is to turn one leg right side out, and slip it inside the other leg—which is still wrong side out—so the right sides are facing each other. Match up the raw edges at the top of the inside leg seam and notches, then pin the legs together all along the crotch seam. You need to leave a gap in the stitching at the front between the small circles for the drawstring opening, so mark these points with some extra pins if you think you'll forget.

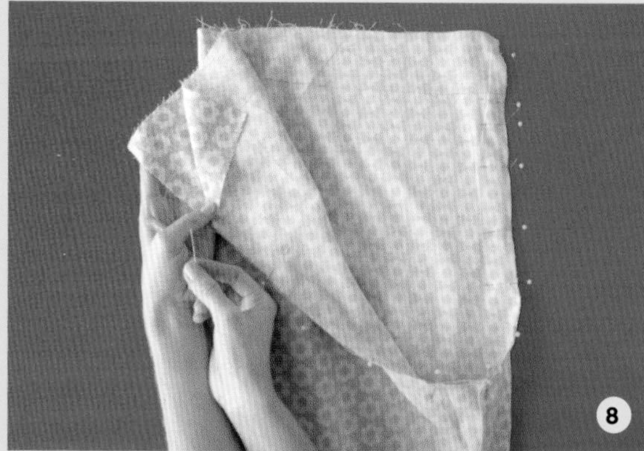
8

9 Stitch the crotch seam. Stitch from the front of the crotch seam to the first drawstring opening marking, backstitching at each end. Snip the threads, then start stitching again from the second marking to the end of the curved seam, again backstitching at each end. If you like to practice yoga in pajamas, the crotch seam can come under a bit of strain over time, so reinforce the middle of the curve with some extra stitches on top of or just inside your first row. Trim the seam allowances. Finish each seam allowance separately using zigzag stitch or an overlocker, and press them open.

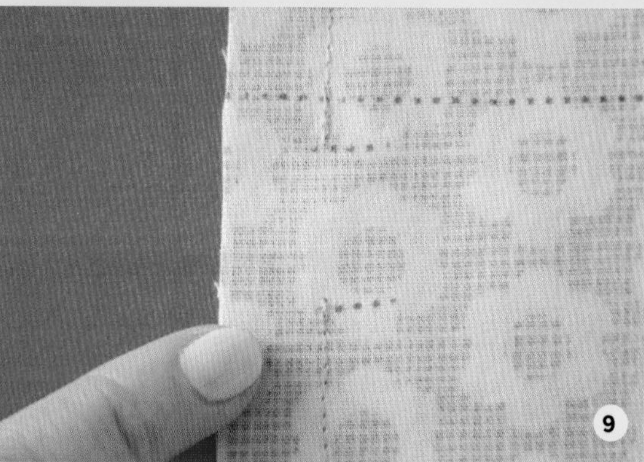
9

10 Reinforce the drawstring opening. Stitch a small rectangle around the drawstring opening on the right side of the fabric to reinforce it. Stitch slowly, pivoting at the corners and making sure the seam allowances stay flat. If you don't yet feel confident enough on the machine, you could sew this part by hand.

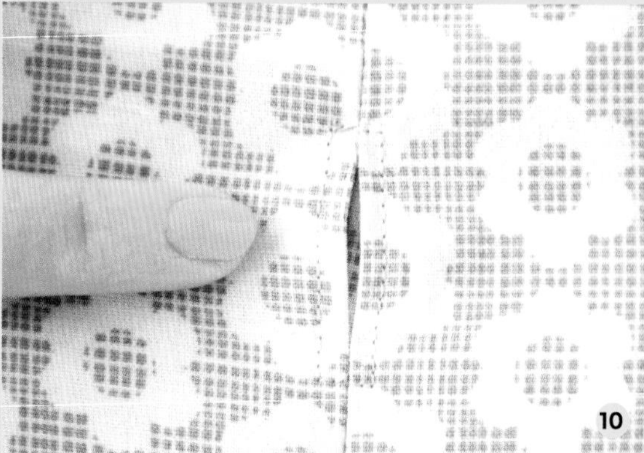
10

SEAM ALLOWANCES

Take care that the pressed leg seam allowances stay folded the right way as you sew over them. If they do get sewn down the wrong way, you can just rip out those few stitches and redo them.

⓫ Make the drawstring channel. Turn ⅜" (1 cm) to the wrong side along the raw edge of the waistline and press. Next, turn this fold to the inside of the pajamas along the marked foldline, press again, and pin in place. Sew right around close to the first pressed fold—you could use the edge of your presser foot as a guide.

⓬ Make a matching drawstring. Place the two long strips right sides together and stitch at one short end. Trim the seam allowances and press them open. Fold the short ends of this joined piece under by ⅝" (1.5 cm), wrong sides together, and press. Fold the strip in half lengthwise, wrong sides together, and press. Open it out again, then fold each raw edge into the center and press. Refold the strip in half lengthwise, enclosing the raw edges, press again, and pin the folded edges together.

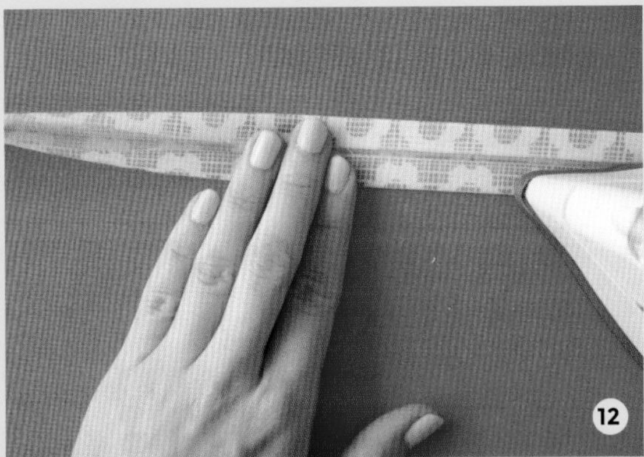

⓭ Sew the drawstring. Stitch along the length of the strip to seal the raw edges in. If you find this part too tricky, you could always use ribbon instead.

SEWING THE DRAWSTRING

Starting right on the edge of a thin strip like this can sometimes result in tangled threads, so start stitching ½" (12 mm) or so from the end, backstitch to the end, then stitch the strip. Finish by backstitching at the other end.

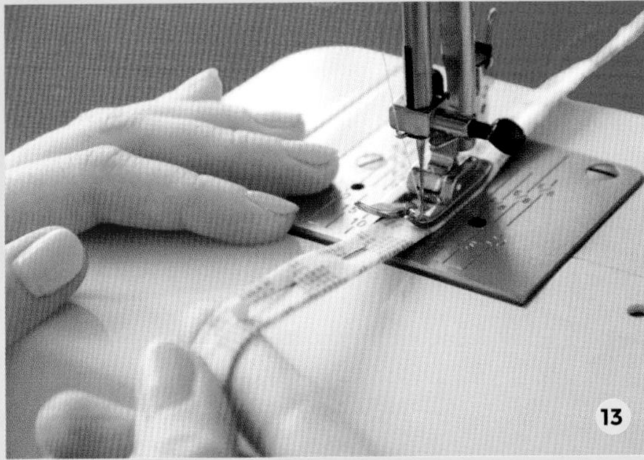

⓮ Thread the drawstring through the channel. Attach a safety pin to one end of the drawstring and use this to thread it through the opening in the front and right around the channel at the top of the pajamas. You can knot the ends of the drawstrings if you like.

⓯ Hem the pajama legs. Hem the pajama legs to the right length (see the Hemming technique, page 60).

HEMMING TECHNIQUE

The final step in making the Margot Pajamas is hemming them. The pattern includes a 1¼" (3 cm) hem allowance. But since we're all different heights, you'll probably want to adjust the length first.

1 Pin the hemline up, try the pajamas on, and adjust the position of the hemline to your preferred length. Take the pajamas off, and fold and press the hemline so it's even, trimming the hem allowance to 1¼" (3 cm) if you've shortened the pajamas.

2 Fold the raw edge under by ⅝" (1.5 cm), press, refold and re-press the hemline, and pin in place. Stitch it close to the inner fold.

Give your pj's a final press, and you're finished! Pajama party time!

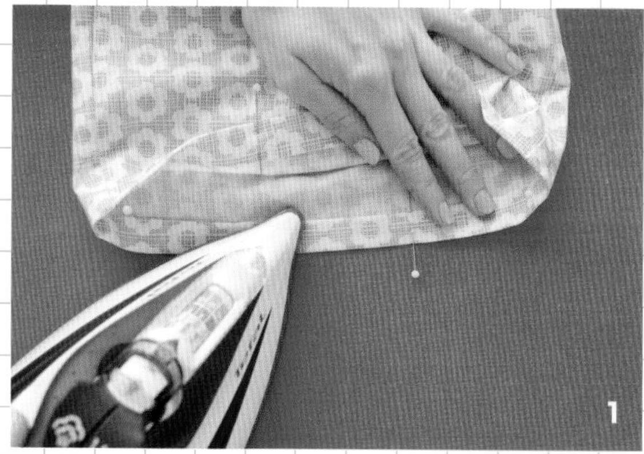

1

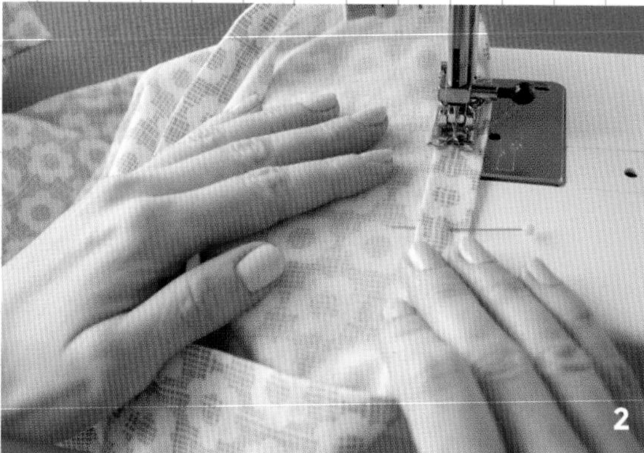

2

SEWING A HEM

Some sewing machines have a removable section of the bed that gives you a free arm, allowing you to loop a leg, sleeve, or other circular area of a garment around it while stitching. Personally, I find I get more control of the fabric without the free arm—by sewing within the loop, wrong side facing up.

MAKE IT YOUR OWN

It's easy to create simple variations of the basic Margot pattern; though beware of making too many comfy pairs of pj's or you'll never want to get out of them.

PATCH POCKET

Add a patch pocket to your Margot Pajamas for stashing candy or simply warming your hand. Make it in a matching or contrasting fabric—it's up to you. Once you've grasped the principle, you can add these pockets to skirts and dresses, too. Sew the pocket on before stitching the pajama pieces together.

1 Cut out a square of fabric measuring 6" x 6" (15 cm x 15 cm). Finish all four sides by zigzagging or overlocking the raw edges. Fold the top edge over by ⅝" (1.5 cm), right sides together, press, and pin. Stitch down the sides of the folded edge only, using a ⅝" (1.5 cm) seam allowance.

2 Clip or fold the corners and turn the fold right side out, easing out the corners into right angles with a pin. Fold the other edges under by ⅝" (1.5 cm) and press.

3 Pin the pocket to one back leg of the pajamas, the wrong side of the pocket against the right side of the pajamas. Rather than pinning it perfectly flat, leave a little bit of space so you can get your hand in. Stitch around three sides, backstitching at the ends and pivoting at the corners, leaving the top edge unstitched. Add some extra stitches at the top of the sides to secure the pocket, in a small triangle shape if you can.

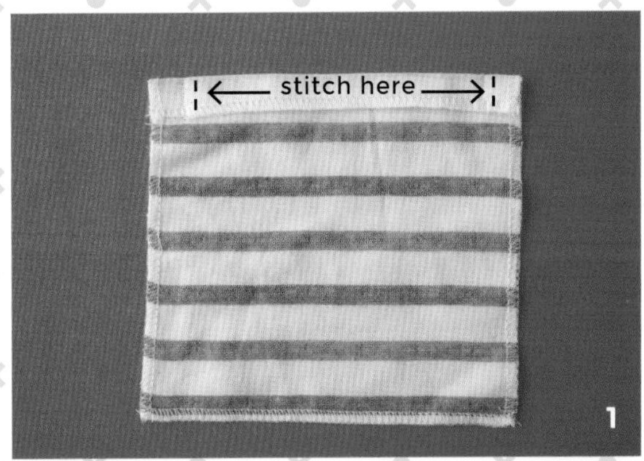

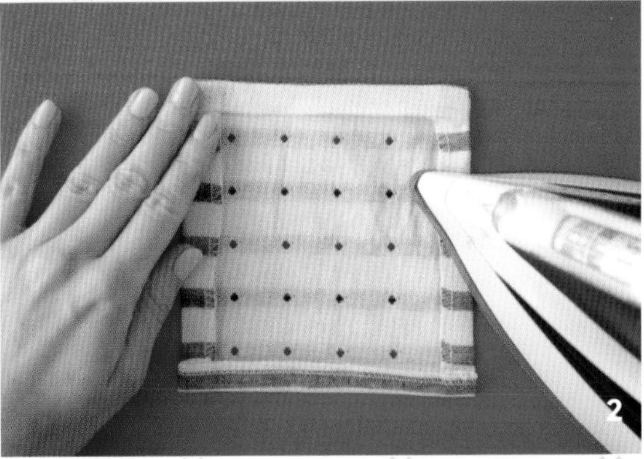

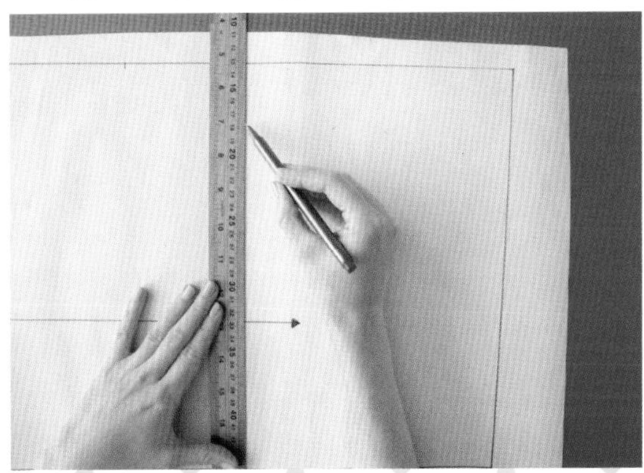

SHORTER LENGTH

Make these pajamas suitable for summer simply by shortening the length of the pattern piece before you cut out the fabric. Be sure to shorten the front and back pieces by the same amount.

SOME MORE IDEAS...

- Tie your pj's with ribbon instead of the drawstring.
- Play around with the shape of the patch pocket.
- Experiment with fancy topstitching (page 36).
- Add pretty piping to the side seams (page 153).
- Insert side-seam pockets for the most practical pj's in the world (page 130).

MAKE IT A LIFESTYLE

HOW TO BEHAVE IN A FABRIC STORE

Ahhh . . . fabric shopping. There's something incredibly therapeutic about entering an emporium of textiles, brimming with roll after roll of material just waiting to be unfurled, discovered, escorted home, and transformed into a dress.

I'll admit I felt a little intimidated the first time I entered a fabric store, not to mention overwhelmed by all the options. What should I ask for? Was I allowed to touch stuff? Would it just be really obvious that I had no clue what I was doing?

Fear not. With a little foresight and insight, fabric shopping can be one of the most fun things you can do with your (homemade) clothes on.

HAVE A STRATEGY

It's so easy to go crazy in a fabric store and spend the GDP of a small country, so stay focused by keeping a list of what you actually need for your sewing projects. I have a list on my phone, with projects I want to make written in the vague order in which I want to tackle them.

For each project, list suitable fabrics, the amount of fabric you need, plus notions such as zippers (and their length), buttons (number and size), interfacing (how heavy?), and thread—don't forget the thread! Picking everything up in one trip will save you a lot of time and hassle.

Try to visualize some ideas for how you'd like the project to look in advance. If you have a shortlist of colors and prints in your head before entering the fabric store, it'll help you stay focused and find exactly what you're after.

If you've already got the fabric and just need the notions, keep a swatch in your bag so you can color match them.

If you're serious about this shopping trip, consider taking a tape measure (for you and the fabric), mirror (for checking colors against your skin tone), and one of those granny shoppers that you can pull along on wheels (to save your back). Seriously! Okay, so I've never gone to these extremes myself, but I've been lucky enough to have accompanied some hardcore shoppers in my time and benefitted greatly from their military-operation-style preparation.

HOW TO ACT LIKE YOU KNOW WHAT YOU'RE DOING

When you enter a fabric store, the first thing to do is to take a deep breath and try not to faint from excitement. Scan the room—get an overview of what's on offer before examining the fabrics.

Fabric is generally kept on rolls or boards. Check the width as this will impact the length of fabric you need.

Don't be afraid to touch stuff. Pull out the roll, unravel a length of the fabric, and get a sense of the texture, thickness, and drape. Imagine how that will translate into your finished garment. (See Choosing Your Fabric on page 44 for more advice on suitable fabrics.)

3 4 5 6
4 3 2

Be honest with yourself about whether you'll wear it. Does the color suit you? Will it go with other things in your wardrobe? Every seamstress has cooed at a kitten-print cotton or two in their time, but would you actually wear it as a dress?

Consider the laundry requirements for your fabric choice. Will it need special care? Is it dry-clean only and, if so, can you be bothered?

Once you've chosen your fabric, a sales assistant can take it up to the table and cut it for you to your required length. Don't be alarmed and yelp in protest if they make a tiny snip and rip the rest—this is standard practice in some stores; they're just tearing along the crosswise grain.

It's a good idea to buy a bit more than your project requires in case you make a mistake. You can always use up that extra bit on a small accessory or contrasting facing.

If you're still not sure, some stores will cut you a sample swatch or two so you can think about it at home. Just don't abuse your swatching privileges! Or if they have a "no samples" policy, you may be able to buy just a very short length.

ADMIT THAT ACTUALLY YOU DON'T KNOW WHAT YOU'RE DOING

When I first went fabric shopping, I excitedly gushed that I was about to take my first sewing class, showed the nice lady the pattern, said I was totally clueless, and asked what fabrics she would recommend. My honesty encouraged her to go out of her way to help me, and she seemed almost as excited as I was.

There's no point pretending you know what you're talking about if you don't. Ask the sales assistants as many questions as you need to—that's what they're there for! Usually they will be delighted to share their knowledge, experience, and passion with you.

THROW THE STRATEGY OUT THE WINDOW

Sometimes you just see a fabric that you fall in love with and no list or spreadsheet can hold you back. Found the perfect Breton stripes? Acquire! Can't stop thinking about that kitten-print cotton? You only live once! It's fine to buy fabric on impulse without a project in mind, as long as you don't mind it sitting in your stash unused for months, if not years, until you match it with the perfect project. Taking over the house with your fabric stash is all part of becoming a DIY dressmaker!

If you don't know what the fabric will be used for, how much should you buy? As a rule of thumb, 2¾ yards (2.5 meters) is generally a safe amount to buy for many projects, or 3¼–4½ yards (3–4 meters) if you're leaning toward a full skirted dress.

AND FINALLY . . .

As soon as you get home, stick your fabric in the wash. Do it now! That way it'll be ready to use tomorrow.

SEWING IS GOOD FOR YOU

DELPHINE SKIRT

CHAPTER 3

Build your everyday handmade wardrobe with the Delphine Skirt, simple to make and incredibly versatile. The exaggerated A-line shape finishes a flirty few inches above the knee, closing at the back with a professional-looking invisible zipper. Tuck in your Mimi Blouse (Chapter 6, pages 138–61) for the office, team it with wool tights for winter, or go for nautical chic with a Breton top and your Brigitte Scarf (Chapter 1, pages 18–39).

SUPPLIES

1 yd (1 m) length of fabric, 60" (150 cm) wide

OR 1½ yd (1.3 m) length of fabric, 45" (115 cm) wide

9" (22 cm) invisible zipper (in color to match your fabric)

Iron-on interfacing (in similar weight to your fabric)

Thread (in color to match your fabric)

TOOLS

See page 14

Zipper foot

Invisible zipper foot

OPTIONAL

Fabric for belt loops (page 86)

Buttons (page 88)

TECHNIQUES

Setting up your sewing machine (page 21)

Stitching school (page 26)

Pinning (page 30)

Adjusting stitches (page 32)

Choosing your fabric (page 44)

Preparing your pattern (page 47)

Laying out fabric and pattern (page 48)

Cutting out fabric pieces (page 50)

Transferring the markings (page 52)

Understanding clothing construction (page 54)

Simple seam allowance finishes (page 55)

Pressing matters (page 57)

Hemming (page 60)

Pattern sizing (page 72)

Understanding ease (page 75)

Interfacing (page 77)

Inserting an invisible zipper (page 80)

FABRIC SUGGESTIONS

Look for a medium-weight to heavyweight fabric with body to hold the A-line shape. Cottons (including gabardine, canvas, and drill), denim, corduroy, or linen will all work well. Even pillow fabric or an old curtain can be used for this skirt!

PATTERN DETAILS

The paper pattern has 4 pieces:
Front skirt—cut 1 on the fold
Back skirt—cut 2
Front waistband—cut 2 on the fold + 1 interfacing
Back waistband—cut 4 + 2 interfacing

Seam allowance is ⅝" (1.5 cm).

PATTERN SIZING

BODY MEASUREMENTS

SIZE	WAIST	HIP
1	24" (61 cm)	33" (84 cm)
2	26" (66 cm)	35" (89 cm)
3	28" (71 cm)	37" (94 cm)
4	30" (76 cm)	39" (99 cm)
5	32" (81 cm)	41" (104 cm)
6	34" (86.5 cm)	43" (109 cm)
7	36" (91.5 cm)	45" (114 cm)
8	38" (96.5 cm)	47" (119.5 cm)

FINISHED GARMENT MEASUREMENTS

SIZE	WAIST	HIP
1	25½" (65 cm)	36" (91.5 cm)
2	27½" (70 cm)	38" (96.5 cm)
3	29½" (75 cm)	40" (101.5 cm)
4	31½" (80 cm)	42" (106.5 cm)
5	33½" (85 cm)	44" (112 cm)
6	35½" (90 cm)	46" (117 cm)
7	37½" (95 cm)	48" (122 cm)
8	39½" (100 cm)	50" (127 cm)

FABRIC LAYOUT

Here is the suggested arrangement of the pattern pieces on the fabric.

back skirt
front waistband
front waistband
fold
selvages
back waistband
back waistband
front skirt

60" (150 cm) wide fabric

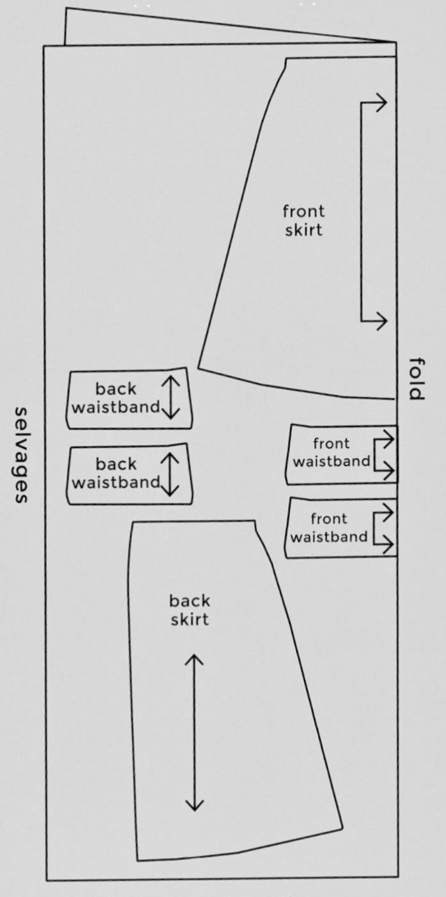

45" (115 cm) wide fabric

PATTERN SIZING

TECHNIQUE

While the Margot Pajamas have a flexible drawstring waist, the Delphine Skirt has a fitted waistband, so you need to start thinking about fitting. This chapter covers the initial steps to achieving a great fit by working with the pattern—taking body measurements, understanding pattern sizing, changing the pattern proportions, and lengthening and shortening pattern pieces. Then Chapter 4 goes into further detail about fitting for more advanced projects (page 96).

TAKING YOUR MEASUREMENTS

The first thing you need to do is to take your body measurements. When you become a whiz at working with and adjusting patterns you may want to note down a whole range of dimensions—high bust, bicep, back width, etc. But for now let's just go with the vital statistics you need in order to pick out your pattern size. Even though the Delphine Skirt doesn't need a bust measurement or back length, we'll include those here because you'll refer back to this section in later projects that do need them.

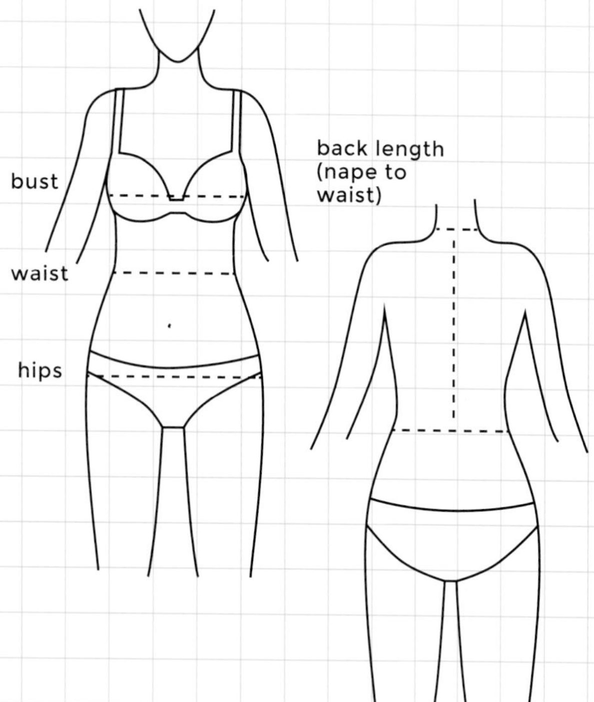

Note down these measurements and keep them somewhere handy:

- **BUST**—the fullest part of your bust, around your nipples.
- **WAIST**—your waistline, or natural waist, is the point at which you bend to the side. For skirts, choose how high or low you want the waistband to sit, and measure at that level.
- **HIP**—the fullest part of your hips.
- **BACK LENGTH**—measure down from the nape of your neck to your natural waist.

I know it can be tempting to breathe in and stick your chest out when a tape measure comes anywhere near you, but there really isn't much point cheating—you'll only end up with uncomfortable clothing! Breathe normally, hold the tape measure level with the floor, and wear only whatever underpants you'll usually wear under the garment you're making. Embrace your unique shape and start getting excited about perfectly fitting garments. Hooray!

SELECT YOUR PATTERN SIZE

Now that you know your body measurements, you need to find your pattern size. Circle your Bust, Waist, and/or Hip measurements (depending on which are listed for the pattern you're using) on the Body Measurements chart at the beginning of the chapter. If you're between sizes, opt for the larger one—you can always take the garment in later.

If your bust-waist-hip ratio corresponds to one of the sizes in the first column, then that's the size you should go for. Your size will be indicated by both numbers and the style of dashed line on the pattern pieces themselves. You may want to draw over these lines in a colored pen to make them easier to see when tracing.

If your bust-waist-hip ratio spans different sizes, that's totally normal! Read the next section for how to get the perfect fit.

COMBINING MULTIPLE PATTERN SIZES

On multisized sewing patterns, such as the ones included in this book, it's easy to mix and match different bust, waist, and hip measurements. And this is precisely one of the reasons why sewing your own clothing is so much better than buying ready-to-wear—you get to make the pattern correspond to your own proportions.

Let's say your waist is 26" (66 cm) and your hips are 39" (99 cm). This makes your pattern size 2 on the waist and size 4 on the hips. Starting with the front skirt or bodice piece of your pattern, use a colored pen to draw a line connecting the size lines at the relevant points—between size 2 waist and size 4 hips in our example. Use a long ruler if the pattern line is straight, or a careful freehand line or shaped ruler if it's curved.

If there's a dart along the line that you are changing (for example, at the bust of the Megan Dress, Mimi Blouse, and Lilou Dress), fold it closed temporarily with tape or pins and roll a tracing wheel over the new line to mark in the dart seams before unfolding the dart again (see page 100 for more on darts).

The colored line you have drawn is your new cutting line. Now repeat the process on the corresponding back pattern piece. Don't forget to mark the notches in, too.

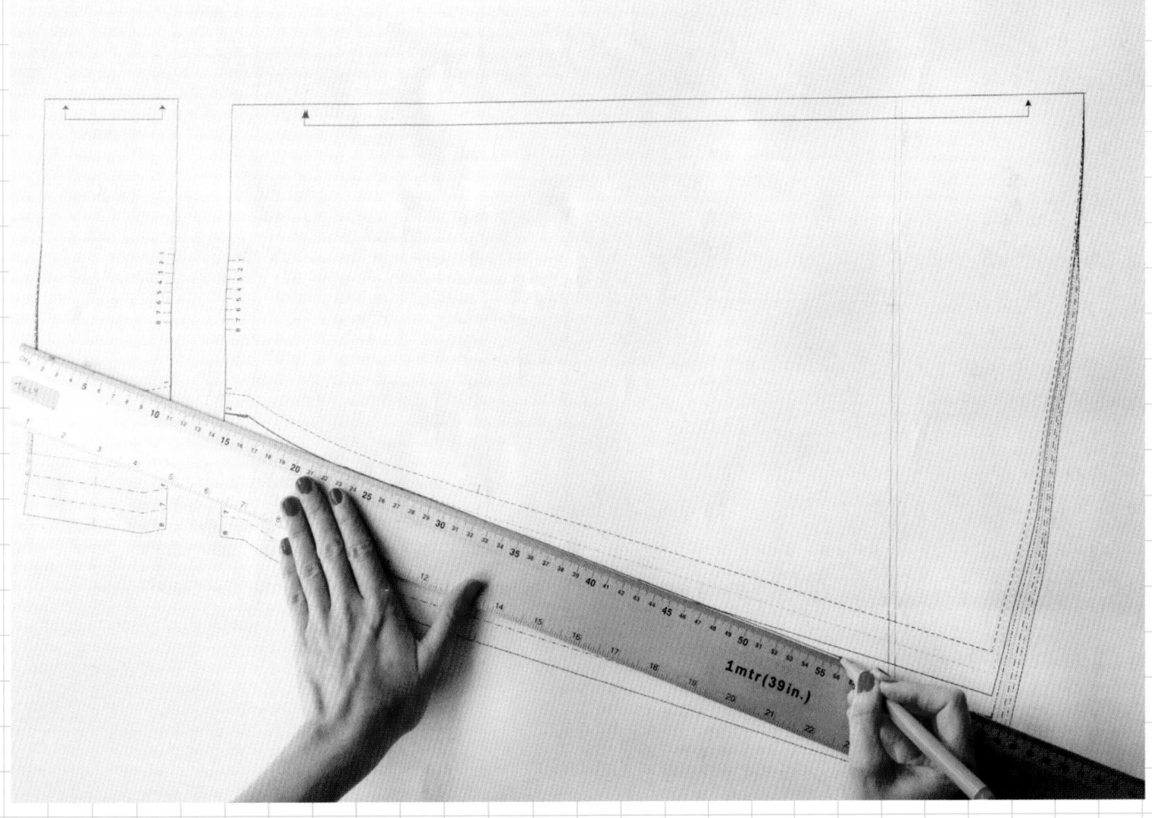

LENGTHENING AND SHORTENING PATTERNS

As well as adjusting the width of your garments, you also have the option to change the length. If you only want to shorten the length by ¾" (2 cm) or so, you can use the hemming method. But if you want to lengthen the garment, shorten it by more than 1" (2.5 cm), or adjust the bodice of a dress, it's better to change the pattern before cutting your fabric. Some pattern pieces include cutting lines specifically for that purpose. Here's how to use them.

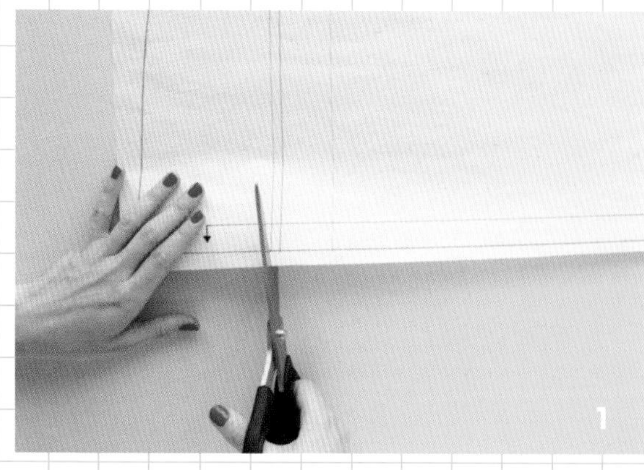

1

2

To lengthen a pattern

1 Trace the front and back skirt/bodice/dress piece of your pattern. Locate the set of double lines where it says "lengthen or shorten here." Cut along one of these lines.

2 On a fresh piece of paper, draw a long straight horizontal line. Measure down by the amount you want to lengthen the pattern, then draw another line parallel to the first one at this point.

3 Place this piece of paper underneath your pattern pieces, taping or gluing the lines you cut on the pattern to the lines you've drawn on the paper.

4 Redraw the pattern side seam to smooth it out. On the Delphine Skirt, draw this line from the hip notch to the hem on both the skirt front and skirt back pattern pieces.

To shorten a pattern

1 Trace the front and back skirt/bodice/dress piece of your pattern. Locate the set of double lines where it says "lengthen or shorten here." Measure up from the upper one by the amount you want to shorten the pattern, then draw a parallel line at this point.

2 Cut along the upper "lengthen or shorten here" line.

3 Overlap the bottom piece on the top piece, taping or gluing the line you cut along to the line you drew.

4 Redraw the pattern side seams on both the front and back pattern pieces.

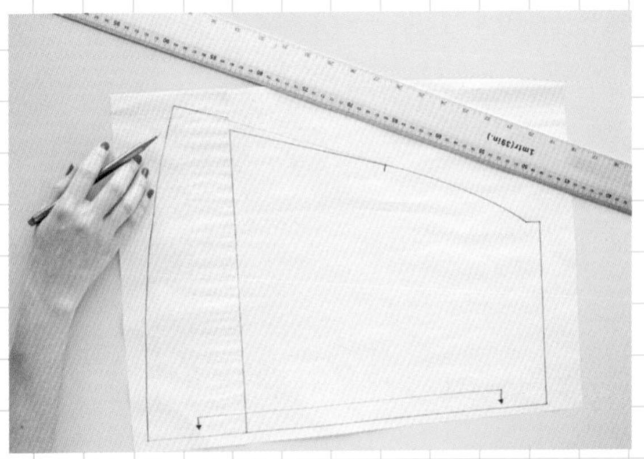

UNDERSTANDING EASE

TECHNIQUE

Have you ever followed the sizing chart on a sewing pattern only to end up with a garment that's too big for you? Many dressmakers encounter this and can't understand where they went wrong. Well fret no more, my friend! Let's get our heads around "ease" to make the process a whole lot . . . erm . . . easier.

Look at the Finished Garment Measurements chart at the beginning of the chapter. Unless you're working in stretch fabrics, these numbers should be larger than the corresponding body measurements. There are two reasons for this. The first and most obvious reason is that the design of the garment may call for it to be wider than your body; for example, on a loose-fitting blouse or the hem of an A-line skirt.

The second reason—and the one that can throw beginner dressmakers—is that even the closest-fitting pattern includes "ease" to allow your body to breathe, move around, and eat lunch. Different sewing pattern brands have their own idea of how much ease is needed, depending on their target market and how comfortable or figure-hugging they want the design to feel.

Personally, I like the following amount of ease for clothes to allow me to breathe like a normal human being without looking frumpy:

- **BUST—**1½–2" (4–5 cm) is the minimum to allow for your ribs to move as you breathe.
- **WAIST—**1–1½" (2.5–4 cm) is just enough to move about a bit and order dessert.
- **HIP—**2" (5 cm) or more ease here will allow you to walk and sit down comfortably in even the closest-fitting skirt.

If you want to know how much ease has been added to a pattern, subtract the numbers on the Body Measurements chart from those on the Finished Garment Measurements chart. If you're using a pattern that doesn't list the finished garment measurements, you can work them out yourself by measuring the pattern and subtracting seam allowances and any darts, pleats, or gathers. (Remember that some of any additional room may be a feature of the garment design.) Now that you know how much extra space there is, you may decide to opt for a different size, depending on how tightly or loosely you like your clothes to fit.

TO MAKE THE SKIRT

❶ **Cut out the paper pattern pieces.** Having selected (and altered if need be) your pattern pieces (see the Pattern Sizing techniques, page 72), pin them to the fabric. Cut out your fabric piece, adding notches and markings, just like you did for the Margot Pajamas.

❷ **Stitch the skirt side seams.** Pin the back skirt pieces to the front skirt at the side seams, right sides together, matching notches. Stitch the side seams.

❸ **Finish the skirt seam allowances.** Trim the seam allowances and finish them with zigzag stitch or an overlocker. Then press them either open or toward the back.

EXTRA NOTCHES
Snip extra notches at the center fold of the front skirt and front waistband pieces to help match them up later.

4 Interface the waistband facing pieces. You should have cut two front waistband pieces and four back waistband pieces. Half of these will form what will be called from now on the "waistband," which will be seen on the outside of the skirt, and the other half will form the "facing," which goes on the inside. Apply interfacing to the wrong side of the waistband pieces—so to one front piece and one left-hand and one right-hand back pieces (see the Interfacing techniques, below).

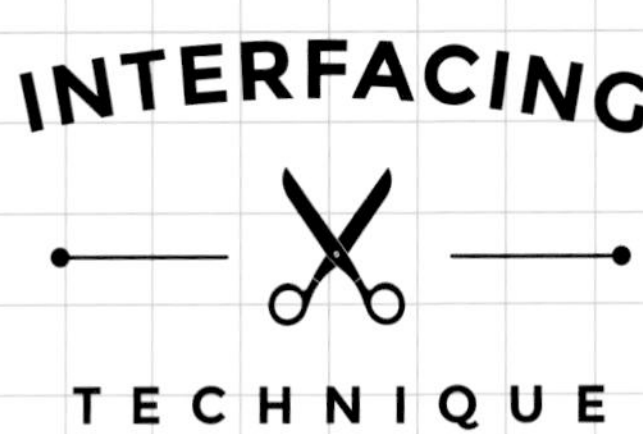

INTERFACING TECHNIQUE

Interfacing is a stiffener added to the parts of a garment that need extra structure or firmness, such as collars, cuffs, waistbands, and facings.

Interfacing can be bought by the yard (meter) or in precut packs; iron-on (sometimes called "fusible") or sew-in; woven, nonwoven (with an almost papery feel), or knit; white or black; lightweight to heavyweight. But the most important thing is that your interfacing is a similar weight to the fabric you're applying it to. (For sheer fabric, which interfacing would show through, you can use a layer of fine fabric such as organza instead.)

My preference is for the iron-on woven stuff, and I keep a stash of lightweight, medium-weight, and heavyweight interfacing so I've always got something suitable on hand. You should always test a small piece of interfacing on a scrap of your fabric first to check what effect it has.

Iron-on interfacing has one smooth side and one rough-feeling side with tiny blobs of glue, which will fuse to your fabric when heated with an iron.

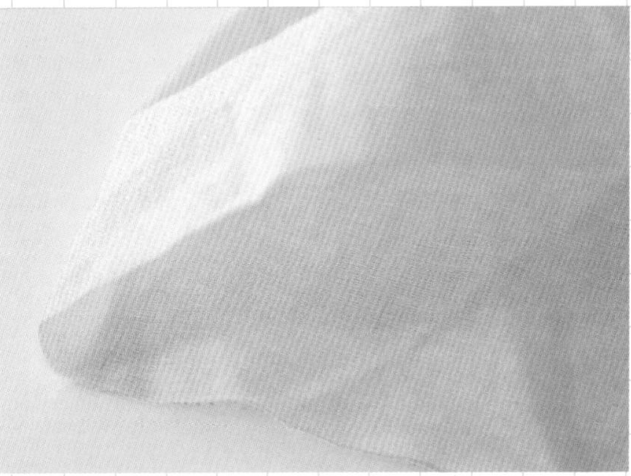

You need to apply interfacing to the Delphine and Clémence Skirt waistbands and the Megan and Mimi neckline facings. The pattern pieces indicate how many pieces of interfacing to cut: for example, "Cut 2 + 1 interfacing" means you should cut two pieces of fabric and one piece of interfacing with that pattern piece. If you're using a different brand of sewing pattern, this instruction is often shortened to "Cut 2 + 1."

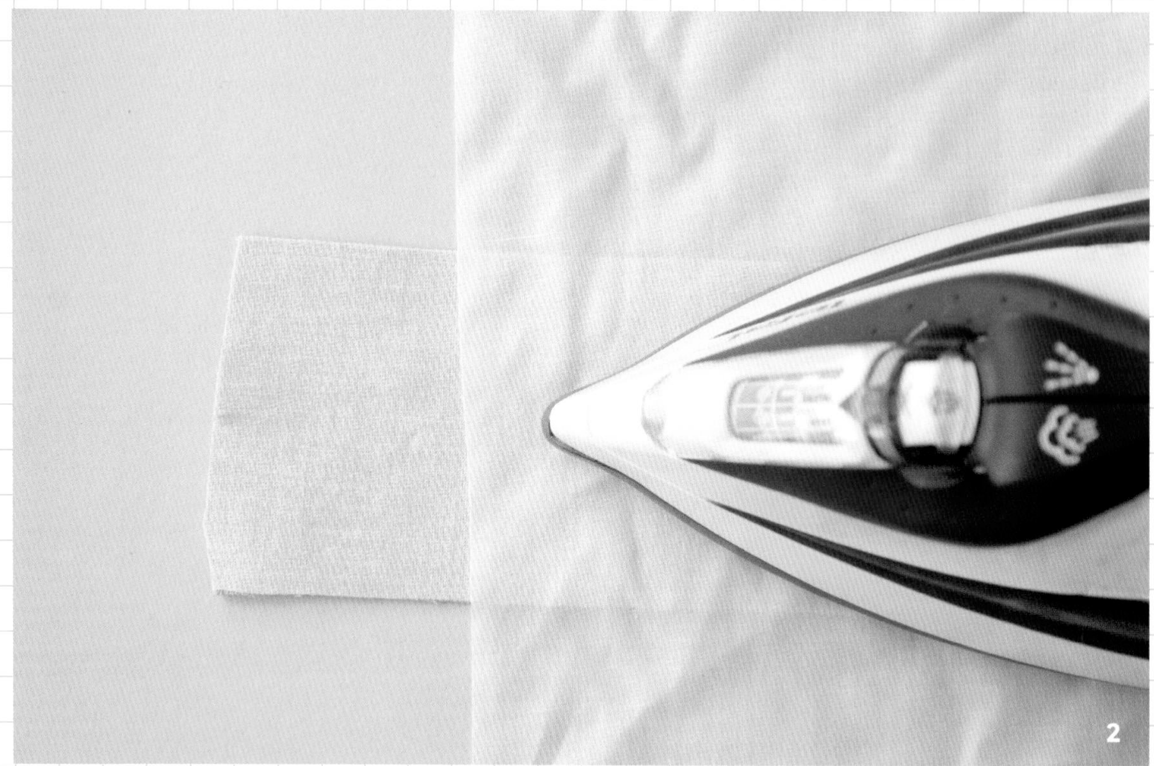

APPLYING IRON-ON INTERFACING

1 Cut the interfacing to the shape of the piece it will be applied to, using your paper pattern piece as a template. Draw in any notches.

REDUCING BULK

If you want to reduce the bulk of your seams, you can cut your interfacing ⅝" (1.5 cm) within the pattern outlines; so along the stitching lines rather than the cutting lines. I must admit I rarely have the patience to do this unless absolutely necessary!

2 Place your fabric piece on an ironing board, wrong side facing up. Position the interfacing piece on top of it, glue side facing down. Place a pressing cloth on top—I use a piece of muslin, or you could use another piece of fabric or even a clean dishtowel. Gently press down onto the fabric with a hot, dry iron for a few seconds to allow the glue to melt and adhere to the fabric. And as if by magic your fabric should now be lovely and stiff.

Be careful that the sticky side of the interfacing doesn't come into contact with your iron or ironing board, or it'll leave a horrible burnt glue mark! Also try not to slide the iron around or the interfacing could get squidged up into a sticky mess—just keep the iron still. (Page 57 has more tips for pressing.)

INTERFACING TRICKS

To interface small, intricate pieces of slippery fabric, cut the shape from the interfacing and press it to the fabric before cutting around it. You'll find it much easier to cut the slippery fabric accurately once it has been interfaced.

5 Construct the skirt waistband. Pin the back waistband pieces to either end of the front waistband at the side seams, right sides together and matching notches. Stitch the side seams. Assemble the facing pieces in the same way.

Trim the seam allowances and press them open with the iron on both the right and wrong sides.

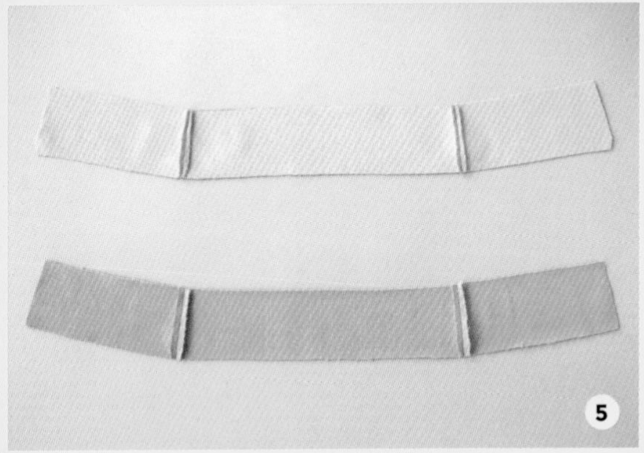

6 Attach the waistband. Pin the bottom edge of the (interfaced) waistband to the top edge of the skirt, right sides together. Make sure the waistband side seams are lying directly on top of the skirt side seams—pin these first, then match the notches before pinning the rest of the waistband. Stitch the waistband to the skirt.

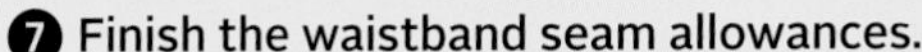

7 Finish the waistband seam allowances. Trim the waistband seam allowances. Press the waistband and the seam allowances up and away from the skirt. Now is a good time to try on the skirt and check if you need to take the center back opening in or out slightly (remember the opening includes a 5/8"/1.5 cm seam allowance on each side).

SEAM ALLOWANCES

Take care that the pressed side seam allowances stay folded the right way as you stitch over them. If they do get sewn down the wrong way, you can just rip out those few stitches and redo them.

If your fabric is fairly thick, trim one seam allowance slightly more than the other. This reduces some of the bulk as the raw edges of the seam allowances won't be lying directly on top of one another: this called "grading seams."

8 Insert the invisible zipper. Insert the zipper into the center back opening of the skirt (see the Inserting an Invisible Zipper technique, page 80), placing the top stop of the zipper 5/8" (1.5 cm) down from the top of the waistband. Stitch the rest of the seam using a regular zipper foot.

INSERTING AN INVISIBLE ZIPPER

TECHNIQUE

The invisible zipper—or the concealed zipper—has an intimidating reputation, but I think that zippers of all kinds can be a little tricky the first time, so you may as well tackle the invisible zipper at the start. It will make your garment look soooo elegant, with the stitching and the zipper teeth hidden away.

To insert an invisible zipper, you will need an invisible zipper foot (on the left) and a regular zipper foot. Some sewing machines come with these included in their accessories tray; otherwise you will need to buy them separately: a worthwhile investment, I promise. Note that the actual zipper itself needs to be an "invisible zipper," one with concealed teeth.

The first time you insert an invisible zipper, it's worth practicing with a spare zipper and fabric before diving into your real garment project. Take a deep breath, focus on what you're doing, and take your time—there's no hurry here. It may not be perfect the first time around, and that's okay. It'll get easier!

1 Turn over ⅝" (1.5 cm) to the wrong side down each center back seam and press in the seamlines. If you want to, you can trim your seam allowances down to the width of the zipper tape. Finish the raw edges using zigzag stitch or an overlocker.

   Open the zipper. With a warm, dry iron, press the back of the zipper to smooth the curled teeth flat. Be careful not to apply a hot iron directly to the teeth—you don't want them to melt!

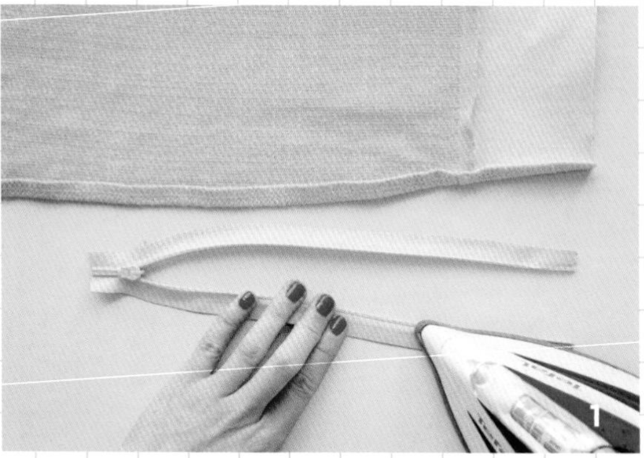

2 Unfold the pressed left-hand back seams. Place the zipper on top of the left-hand opening, right sides together, with the teeth of the left-hand zipper tape aligned with the pressed seamline, and the left-hand zipper tape sitting within the seam allowance. The top stop of the zipper should be ⅝" (1.5 cm) down from the top of the waistband. Pin the zipper in place.

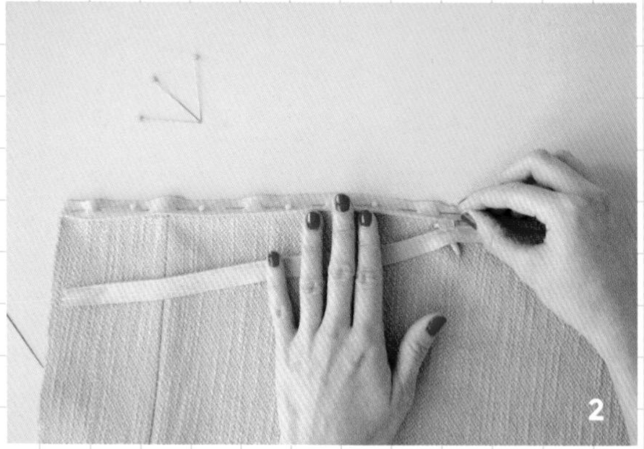

3 Attach an invisible zipper foot to your machine. Slot the teeth of the left-hand zipper tape into the left-hand groove of the foot and, with the needle on the tape side, stitch the zipper to the fabric, close to (but not over!) the teeth. Start sewing from the top (don't forget to backstitch) and stitch as far as you can before reaching the zipper pull. This can seem a bit tricky, but hold both the zipper and fabric taut to avoid rippling, take your time, and you'll be fine. Backstitch at the end and snip the threads as short as possible so they don't get caught in the zipper.

4 Close the zipper and align the right-hand waistline seam with the left-hand one, keeping it in place with a pin through the right zipper tape. Open the zipper and pin the entire length of the right-hand zipper tape in place, matching the teeth to the pressed seamline as for the left-hand tape. Stitch in place, with the teeth of the right-hand zipper tape in the right-hand groove of the foot.

STABILIZING THE SEAM ALLOWANCES

Applying a strip of interfacing to the seam allowances you'll be attaching the zipper tapes to can help prevent the fabric from puckering.

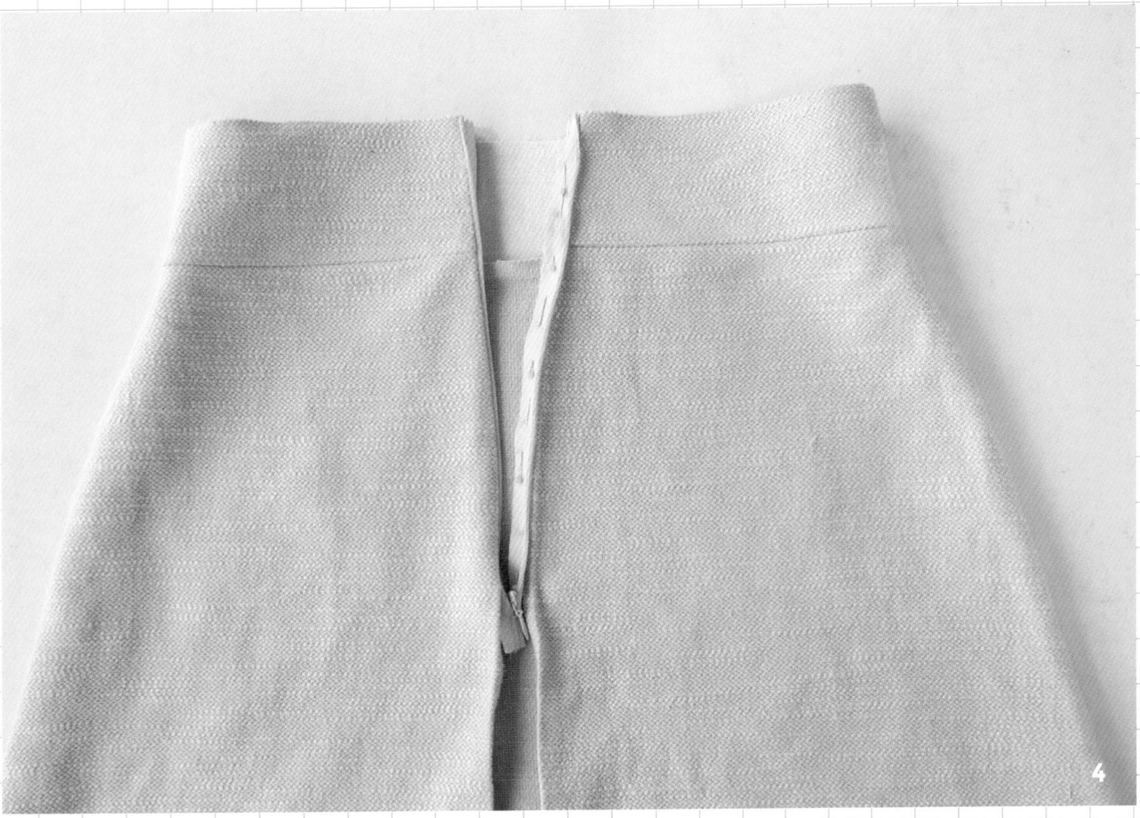

MATCHING SEAMS

If you want to make extra sure that your right-hand waistline seam is going to match up with the left-hand one, sew a few stitches over this bit first. Close the zipper and check that the seams match before attaching the rest of the right-hand zipper tape.

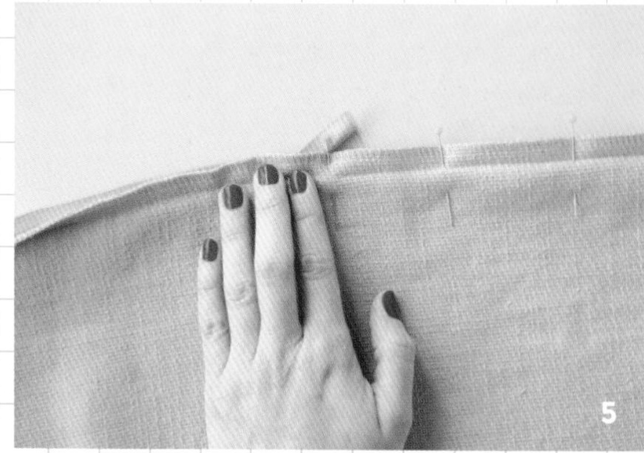

5

5 To stitch the rest of the seam, first close the zipper. With the ends of the zipper tapes pushed out of the way, pin the remainder of the center back seams together.

6 Attach a standard zipper foot to your machine. Start stitching about ¾" (2 cm) above the end of the line of zipper stitching, all the way to the bottom of the seam, being careful not to catch the zipper tapes. The trick is to stitch as close as you can to the line of zipper stitching so the gap doesn't leave a dodgy-looking bump at the bottom of the zipper.

7 At the bottom of the zipper, hand sew the bottom flappy ends of the zipper tapes to the seam allowances.

8 Press the seam allowances open on both wrong and right sides, without touching the zipper with the iron. You will only see the pull at the top, the rest of the zipper is concealed. Nice!

8

How did you get on? The more invisible zippers you insert, the neater they'll get!

9 Attach the facing to the skirt waistband. Press ⅝" (1.5 cm) to the wrong side along the bottom edge of the facing.

Open the zipper. Pin the skirt waistband to the facing along the top edges, right sides together, matching side seams and notches. At the center back, catch the zipper tape between waistband and facing, and pin in place.

Attach a zipper foot to your machine. Stitch the waistband to the facing at the center back seams, close to the zipper teeth—the bottom edge of the facing should still be turned under.

Reattach a regular presser foot. Stitch the waistband to the facing along the top edge.

9

SEWING INTERFACED PIECES

Sometimes when stitching interfaced and noninterfaced pieces of fabric together, one ends up shorter than the other. Stitching with the interfaced piece on top can help prevent this.

10

10 Trim the seam allowances. Trim the seam allowances down to ¼" (5 mm). Using the tip of the iron, press the seam allowances open as far as you can to help define a neat seamline.

11 Fold the waistband facing right side out. Starting with the corners at the top of the center back opening, fold one set of seam allowances toward the garment and fold the other set on top of them to form a square at the corner. Holding the corner in place with your finger, turn the garment right side out.

Use a pin on the right side to gently tease out the fabric into a nice looking corner. Be careful not to poke a hole in it though!

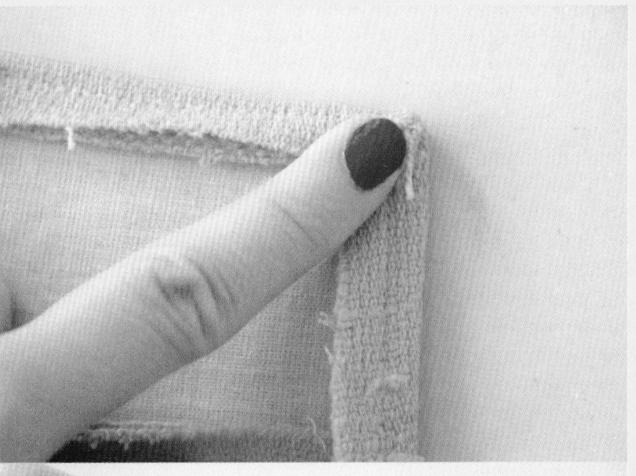

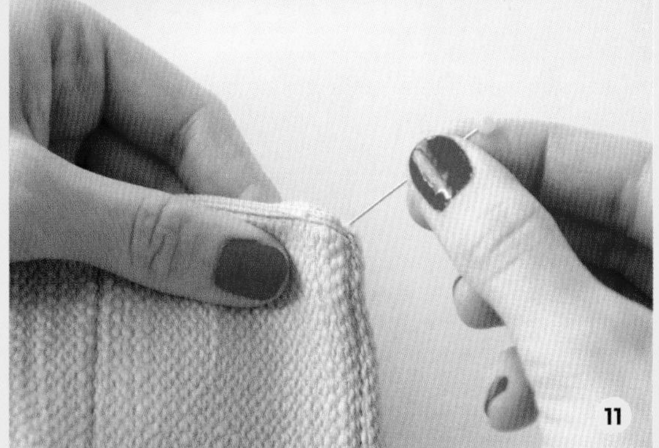
11

MAKING NEAT CORNERS

Sewing patterns often tell you to snip a corner before turning. While this technique can be useful on bulkier fabrics, folding the corner instead will keep it neat and sturdy, and less susceptible to developing a hole.

12 Press the waistband. Press the waistband from the wrong side, rolling the seam along the top slightly toward the inside of the garment so it's not visible from the outside.

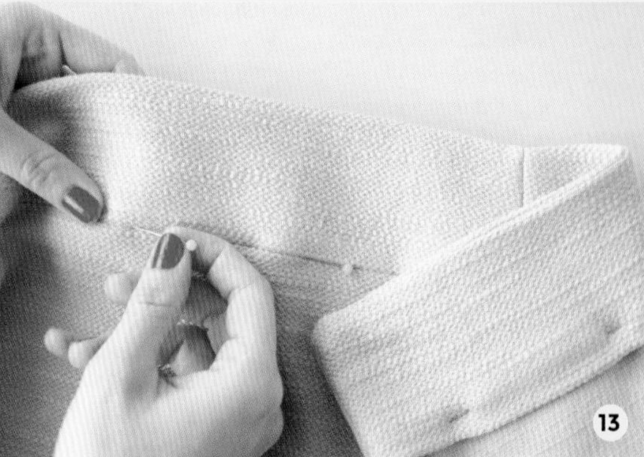

STEAMING SEAMS

Use a little steam from your iron to soften the seamline to help you roll it to the inside with your fingers.

13 Stitch the facing to the inside of the skirt. Pin the bottom edge of the facing to the inside of the skirt, pinning from the right side of the skirt. On the right side, topstitch the waistband close to the seamline to stitch it to the facing. Alternatively, if you don't want the stitches to be seen, you could stitch in the ditch (page 128), or slipstitch the facing down by hand (page 173).

14 Hem the skirt. The Delphine Skirt includes a 1¼" (3 cm) hem allowance. Fold under by ⅝" (1.5 cm) and press. Fold under by another ⅝" (1.5 cm), press, and pin. Try the skirt on and adjust the hemline if you prefer. Topstitch the hem in place, close to the first fold.

Give everything a final press and your Delphine Skirt is done! Woop!

STICKING ZIPPER

Sometimes an invisible zipper can get stuck at the waistline when you try to do it up. If your fabric is fairly thick, reduce the bulk at the waistline by clipping out corners on some of the seams.

MAKE IT YOUR OWN

The Delphine Skirt is so versatile you can make it again and again, with a different look each time. Here are some ideas . . .

BELT LOOPS

Attach belt loops to the waistband before sewing it to the skirt.

1 To make four belt loops ½" (12 mm) wide, cut a long strip of fabric parallel to the selvages, about 16" (40 cm) long by 2" (5 cm) wide.

2 Press the strip in half lengthwise. Open it out again, then fold each raw edge into the center and press. Refold the strip in half lengthwise, enclosing the raw edges, press again, and pin the layers together.

3 Topstitch down each side of the length of the strip, close to the edges. Cut the strip into four equal lengths. For the Delphine Skirt, the strips each need to be 3¾" (9.5 cm) long.

1

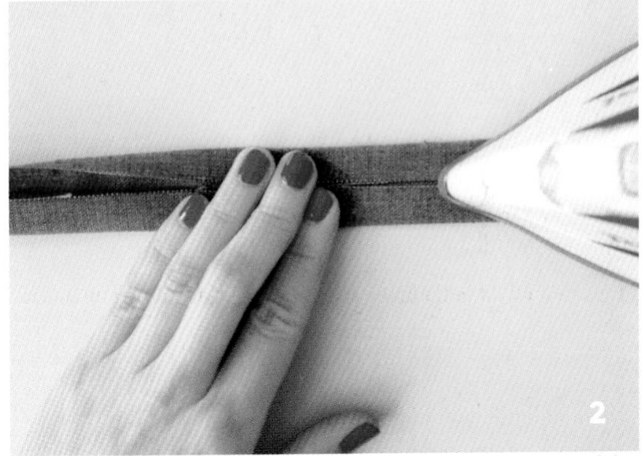
2

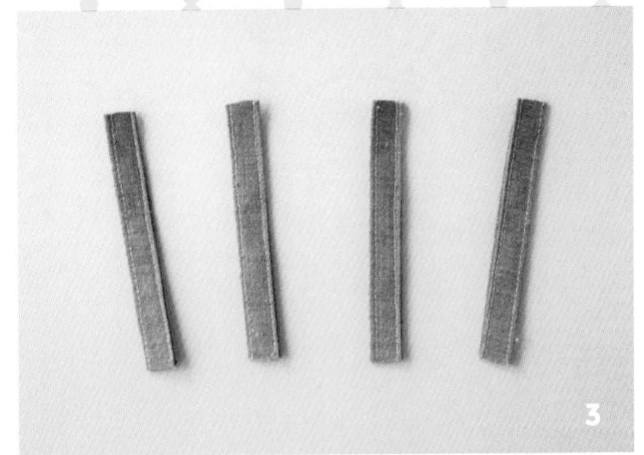
3

4 Position the belt loops where you want them to sit on the right side of the waistband. Align the raw edges of the belt loops with the raw edges of the waistband (the loops are slightly longer than the width of the waistband to accommodate the belt). Machine-baste in place close to the raw edges.

You can now attach the waistband to the skirt following the instructions.

SOME MORE IDEAS...

- Insert piping along the waistband seam (page 152).
- Make the waistband facing in a contrasting fabric.
- Create a faux button tab.
- Add side-seam pockets (page 130) for carrying essential candy.
- Hand embroider a design onto the waistband.

DECORATE WITH BUTTONS

Hand sew buttons onto the front of the skirt. Play around with the positioning to create your own design—try a line of buttons all the way down one side of the skirt, or two buttons on the waistband only (see page 151 for tips on sewing on buttons).

CREATING AN INSPIRING SEWING SPACE

Whether you're sewing on the kitchen table or in your very own craft room, you'll want to make your space both practical and pretty. Having easy access to your tools, keeping things organized, and having a beautiful space that inspires you to create can make a huge difference to your sewing productivity.

THE SETTING

Having a dedicated sewing space is ideal, whether that means commandeering a spare room or simply setting up a small table in the corner of the living room. Leaving your stuff out means you can get sucked into your latest project right away whenever the urge strikes. If you are sharing your sewing space with the kitchen table, keep all your everyday sewing tools in a box that you can pull out and clear away quickly and easily.

Make sure you have enough light so you can see your stitching clearly. Be kind to your eyes by sewing near a window during the daytime and investing in a decent lamp for sewing through the dark winter evenings.

Vacuuming thread off the carpet is not fun. So if you can cut your fabric or sew in a room with a floor that's sweepable, that's a bonus!

ORGANIZING FABRIC

Over time you're bound to build up a stash of lovely fabric, so keeping it organized will make your life a little easier. I like to keep my fabric on shelves so I can see it easily, rolled rather than folded so I can pull it out and put it away without messing up the rest of the stash. You could organize it by type of fabric, or by color for a lovely rainbow effect. If you're super organized, it's a great idea to staple a little note to a corner of each roll, detailing the type of fabric, the length, where you bought it, and any special laundry requirements.

If you do have fabric on open shelves, do be sure that it's not in the sun. Sunlight can fade fabric alarmingly quickly, and it's very depressing to unfold a length and discover a pale stripe across it.

STORING SEWING PATTERNS

You'll probably start building up a sewing pattern collection before too long, so consider how to store them. Some people like to keep them on a bookshelf so they can be pulled out easily, or you could keep them in a plastic or cardboard box to keep the dust off. If you have vintage sewing patterns, sealing them in individual, acid-free, magazine-collector bags and storing them in an archive box will help conserve them.

SORTING TOOLS AND NOTIONS

Keep all your sewing paraphernalia organized so you know where everything is, and it's within easy reach when you need it. Store zippers, buttons,

and trimmings in separate jars or pretty tin boxes. A toolbox or small drawer unit can be great for keeping scissors, marking tools, and pressing aids, or you could mount a pegboard or hook rack on the wall to display them with pride. A thread rack is a great way of keeping your spools organized—and the rainbow display looks so pretty!

DECORATION

I'm a big fan of online pinboards, and real-life ones can be just as great for giving you design ideas and keeping you motivated to create. Try mounting an inspiration board above your sewing space to display images with a look or mood that you want to re-create in your projects. Or how about framing those vintage patterns? They're works of art!

MEGAN DRESS

CHAPTER 4

Megan is the perfect little staple dress that you'll want to make again and again. The high waistline bodice is elegantly shaped with both darts and dart tucks, flowing into a super-flattering semi-fitted skirt that skims over the curves. The fit of the skirt is comfortable and generous enough so you can run for the bus or bop at the disco. The dress has short sleeves and closes at the back with an invisible zipper. This pattern is just calling out for cute prints, embellishments, or color blocking!

SUPPLIES

1⅝ yd (1.5 m) length of fabric, 60" (150 cm) wide
OR 2½ yd (2.3 m) length of fabric, 45" (115 cm) wide
22" (56 cm) invisible zipper (in color to match your fabric)
Iron-on interfacing (in similar weight to your fabric)
Thread (in color to match your fabric)

TOOLS

See page 14
Zipper foot
Invisible zipper foot

OPTIONAL

Contrasting fabric and three buttons for faux placket (page 110)
Ribbon trimming (page 112)

TECHNIQUES

Setting up your sewing machine (page 21)
Stitching school (page 26)
Pinning (page 30)
Adjusting stitches (page 32)
Choosing your fabric (page 44)
Preparing your pattern (page 47)
Laying out fabric and pattern (page 48)
Cutting out fabric pieces (page 50)
Transferring the markings (page 52)
Understanding clothing construction (page 54)
Simple seam allowance finishes (page 55)
Pressing matters (page 57)
Hemming (page 60)
Pattern sizing (page 72)
Understanding ease (page 75)
Interfacing (page 77)
Inserting an invisible zipper (page 80)
Fitting your garment (page 96)
Staystitching (page 99)
Shaping with darts and dart tucks (page 100)
Attaching a neckline facing (page 104)
Setting in sleeves (page 106)
Gathering (page 125)

FABRIC SUGGESTIONS

Choose a medium-weight fabric with enough body to hold the shape of the dress but that won't restrict movement. Try medium-weight cottons (including poplin, twill, sateen, and quilting cottons), lightweight linen, double knit, or medium-weight crepe.

PATTERN DETAILS

The paper pattern has 7 pieces:
Front bodice—cut 1 on the fold
Back bodice—cut 2
Front skirt—cut 1 on the fold
Back skirt—cut 2
Front neckline facing—cut 1 on the fold + 1 interfacing
Back neckline facing—cut 2 + 2 interfacing
Sleeve—cut 2

Seam allowance is ⅝" (1.5 cm).

PATTERN SIZING

BODY MEASUREMENTS

SIZE	BUST	WAIST	HIP
1	30" (76 cm)	24" (61 cm)	33" (84 cm)
2	32" (81 cm)	26" (66 cm)	35" (89 cm)
3	34" (86.5 cm)	28" (71 cm)	37" (94 cm)
4	36" (91.5 cm)	30" (76 cm)	39" (99 cm)
5	38" (96.5 cm)	32" (81 cm)	41" (104 cm)
6	40" (101.5 cm)	34" (86.5 cm)	43" (109 cm)
7	42" (106.5 cm)	36" (91.5 cm)	45" (114 cm)
8	44" (112 cm)	38" (96.5 cm)	47" (119.5 cm)

FINISHED GARMENT MEASUREMENTS

SIZE	BUST	WAIST	HIP
1	31½" (80 cm)	28" (71 cm)	37½" (95 cm)
2	33½" (85 cm)	30" (76 cm)	39½" (100.5 cm)
3	35½" (90 cm)	32" (81 cm)	41½" (106 cm)
4	37½" (95 cm)	34" (86.5 cm)	43½" (111 cm)
5	39½" (100 cm)	36" (91.5 cm)	45½" (116 cm)
6	41½" (105.5 cm)	38" (96.5 cm)	47½" (121 cm)
7	43½" (110.5 cm)	40" (101.5 cm)	49½" (126 cm)
8	45½" (115.5 cm)	42" (106.5 cm)	51½" (131 cm)

FABRIC LAYOUT

Here is the suggested arrangement of the pattern pieces on the fabric.

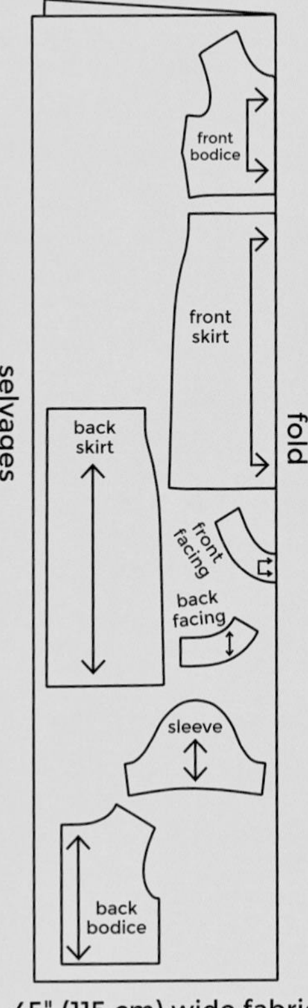

45" (115 cm) wide fabric

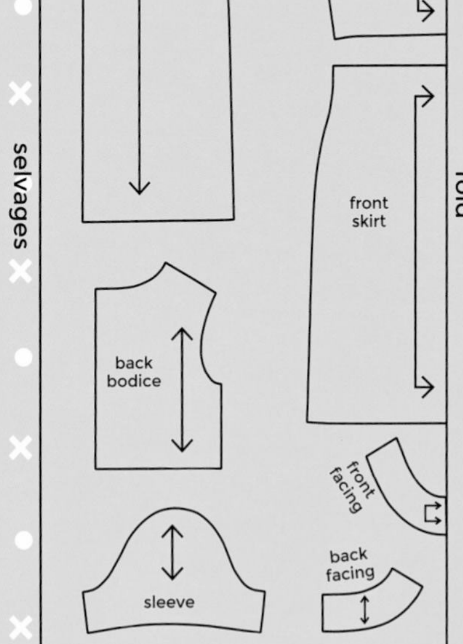

60" (150 cm) wide fabric

TO MAKE THE DRESS

❶ **Make any alterations needed to the paper pattern pieces to fit your shape.** Cut and baste together a toile of the bodice, plus one sleeve, and the skirt if you want to. Adjust the toile to fit your shape, then transfer the changes to your paper pattern pieces (see the Fitting Your Garment technique, below).

FITTING YOUR GARMENT

TECHNIQUE

One of the best things about becoming your own dressmaker is acquiring the power to make clothes that fit your unique shape, rather than trying to fit your body into off-the-rack clothes made for an "average" figure. Take a look around at all the different body types out there, with different bust-waist-hip ratios, curves protruding at different places and in different directions, different torso and leg lengths. When you think of how much diversity there is in body shape, the idea of a standard "size 6" doesn't really mean that much. Making your own clothes means that you can change the shape of the garment to fit you much better than most ready-to-wear clothing will. A sewing pattern is like a template—it has been drafted to a particular shape that you can adapt so that the clothes you make from it fit you just as you'd like them to.

Fitting is a massive topic, with whole books and websites dedicated to it. But the good news is that you don't need to know it all—if you're making clothes for yourself, you'll only have to get to grips with a small number of adjustments. Get to know your body and you'll soon learn which changes you need to make. For example, I know that I always need to shorten the length of the bodice, narrow the shoulders, and grade to a larger hip size. Once I figured this out, I was able to start making these alterations to the patterns that I work with, and fitting myself is no longer such a headache. In this section the fitting process and some common adjustments are discussed, but there isn't space in this book to cover everyone's fitting needs, so I've suggested further reading on page 184.

Grading between different-size patterns and lengthening or shortening patterns has already been covered. In this and subsequent chapters, the patterns become a little more involved to fit, so you'll get an overview of the fitting process, plus when and how to make and adjust a toile.

THE FITTING PROCESS

If you're not sure where to start with fitting, you may want to follow these steps.

1 Compare your body measurements to the finished garment measurements and make any necessary changes to the pattern itself.
   - Combining pattern sizes to your bust-waist-hip proportion.
   - Lengthening or shortening the bodice or skirt for a tall or short torso or legs.
   - Other adjustments you may need for your particular shape, such as small or full bust, swayback, sloping shoulders. (See page 184 for suggested further reading.)

2 Optional: make a toile (see right), adjust it to fit you, and transfer these changes to the pattern pieces. You may then need to make a second toile to check the amended pattern, too.

3 Cut your fabric to your adjusted pattern.

4 Pin or baste the darts and seams together before stitching to double check the fit—this step is particularly recommended if you haven't made a toile! Make any adjustments, then stitch away.

MAKING A TOILE

A toile (pronounced "twal," and sometimes called a muslin) is a mock version of a garment, or part of a garment, constructed in order to check and adjust the fit before you cut into your nice garment fabric.

You don't always need to make a toile, but it's a good idea to make one if the garment is fitted or if it looks like it could need more changes than simply adjusting the side seams. You don't necessarily need to toile the whole garment either, only the parts that may need changing—such as the bodice, one of the sleeves, and/or a fitted skirt such as a pencil skirt. Don't worry about making collars, facings, or other details at this stage unless you think you may want to change their shape, too. You don't need to insert zippers or buttonholes either—just pin any closures together.

A toile is often made out of unbleached calico cotton. Alternatively, you can use an old sheet or some cheap fabric that you don't mind cutting up. Choose a fabric with a similar weight and drape to your garment fabric, as this will make a difference in the way the garment fits and hangs. It's a good idea to pick something light in color so you can draw changes on it. Baste the toile together in a contrasting thread, try it on, and assess the fit in a mirror (or two mirrors!).

Now make any changes to the toile until you're happy with the fit. Some common adjustments are outlined on page 98, or I'd recommend consulting a dedicated fitting resource if your issue isn't covered here. Transfer your changes back to the pattern before cutting your fabric. Now that you've made your fitting adjustments, it will be soooo much quicker to make the garment next time!

Finally, if the thought of spending all that time sewing a toile without getting any wear out of it fills you with horror, consider making what is known by home dressmakers as a wearable toile. This is a full first version of the garment made in cheap—but wearable—fabric, sewn together as per the pattern instructions. The idea is that you end up with both a toile to inform any pattern changes and a garment that you can at least wear around the house!

ADJUSTMENTS TO THE TOILE

Here are some common adjustments you may need, depending on your shape:

Adjusting seams

Sometimes getting a better fit is just a matter of moving seamlines. Try taking the sides, center back, or arms in or out, using pins to test where the new seamline should be—just remember that the stitching lines are ⅝" (1.5 cm) away from the cutting lines. Once you're happy, cut your real garment to the new cutting lines (⅝"/1.5 cm away from the stitching lines) and sew your garment together. You can also use this technique to move a waistline up or down, or to take shoulders in or out.

Altering necklines

What if you want a higher or lower neckline? Draw in the neckline you want on the toile, making sure it's smooth and symmetrical, and matching up the front and back necklines at the shoulder seams. Beware of changing a neckline too much as a lower neckline requires a slightly different shape of bodice than a higher one to avoid sagging. If the garment has a neckline facing, you'll need to adjust that to match. Before you transfer the changes back to your pattern and cut your fabric, don't forget to add an extra ⅝" (1.5 cm) for the seam allowance.

Repositioning darts

Darts can be changed in size and moved up or down to fit your silhouette. When fitting a bust dart, the tip should point toward the nipple, usually stopping about 1" (2.5 cm) away to avoid the bullet-bra look (yikes!). Try repositioning darts on a toile in the first instance, but if the garment is still not fitting your bust, you may need to make a full or small bust adjustment to the pattern (there are lots of tutorials for this online, or take a look at the recommended resources on page 184).

Adding or removing fabric

You might need to add or take away some fabric somewhere more central, such as in the middle of a bodice, where the toile is showing excess tightness or bagginess. To add fabric, cut along the place you think you need more room, spread the toile open and pin a small scrap of fabric underneath the gap. To remove fabric, pinch it out with your fingers and pin together. Once you're happy with the toile, make the same changes to the pattern pieces with paper and tape.

Underarm fit

If you have trouble moving your arms in the sleeves, it could be because the underarm seam is too low for you. Redraw the bottom curve of the armhole on both front and back bodice pattern pieces so it is slightly higher up. The ease in the sleeve will usually allow you to get away with small changes like this without having to adjust the sleeve too, but do check it on a toile first.

2 Cut out your fabric dress pieces with your (adjusted) pattern. Transfer markings and snip notches in the seam allowance in the center of the neckline of the front bodice and front facing.

3 Staystitch the neckline. Staystitch the neckline edge on the front and back bodice pieces (see the Staystitching technique, below).

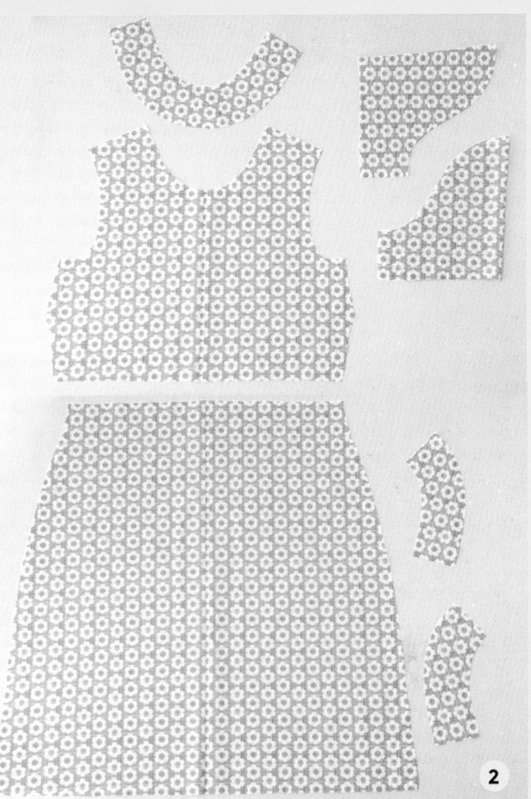

STAYSTITCHING

TECHNIQUE

Staystitching is a row of machine stitches sewn on a single layer of fabric to help it keep its shape. It is added just after the fabric piece has been cut and before it has been attached to anything else. Staystitching diagonal or curved seamlines—such as the neckline of dresses and blouses—can help prevent the fabric from stretching. Staystitching across folds of fabric, such as the pleats on the Lilou Dress (page 162), will help hold them in place.

To staystitch, simply machine stitch parallel to the cutting line within the seam allowance—stitch about ⅜" (1 cm) from the edge. When staystitching a symmetrical curve, such as the front neckline on the Megan and Lilou Dresses, stitch from one shoulder to the center, then from the other shoulder to the center.

4 Stitch all the darts and dart tucks on the dress bodice pieces. There are two darts and two dart tucks on the front bodice and one dart on each back bodice piece. Press the horizontal bust darts downward and the vertical waistline darts and dart tucks toward the center on both wrong and right sides of the fabric, avoiding pressing the folds above the dart tucks (see the Shaping with darts and dart tucks technique, below).

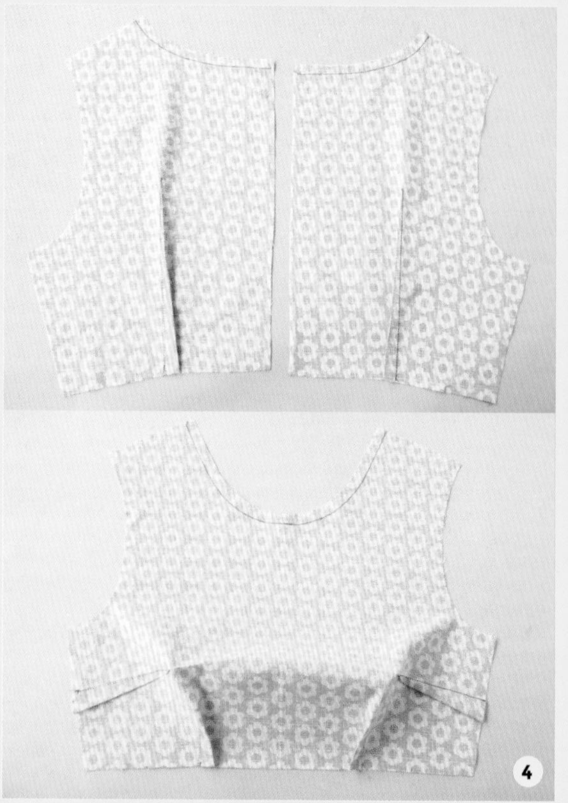

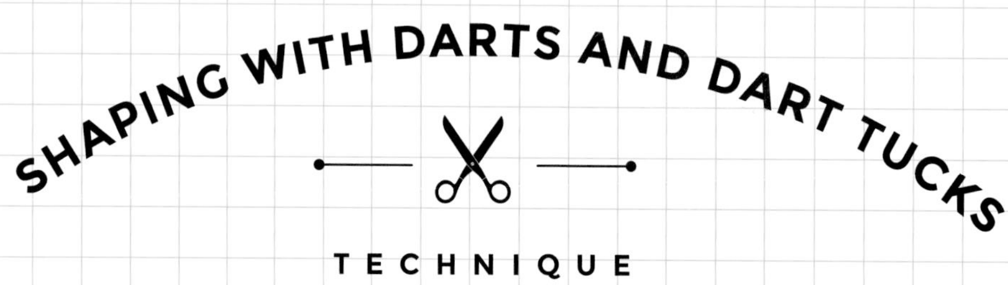

SHAPING WITH DARTS AND DART TUCKS

TECHNIQUE

Darts and dart tucks are folds of fabric sewn down to create a three-dimensional form out of fabric, helping it to fit around the curves of the body. Darts can be straight or curved, single-pointed or double-pointed. In this book we're going to focus on the most common kind of dart, the straight and single-pointed variety, as well as a softer dart tuck, which is a bit like half a dart.

You should have transferred the dart and tuck markings to the wrong side of your fabric pieces when you cut them out—these lines are the dart "legs." Note that the shape of some of the darts begins with a vertical line and turns into a diagonal line. I also like to draw in a third line to mark the center of the dart, as this makes it easier to fold the dart accurately.

TO STITCH A DART

1 Make sure your darts are clearly marked. Then fold along the center line, right sides together, bringing one dart leg directly on top of the other, and pin. Press along the center line.

> **PINNING DARTS**
> If you pin exactly along one of the dart legs, you can check that the other side is aligned accurately.

2 Stitch along the dart legs, starting from the raw edge of the fabric, backstitching at the start, then stitching toward the dart tip. (If you start stitching at the tip, your thread is susceptible to getting knotted into a big mess.) Stitch as straight as you can. Many dart legs are single straight lines, but look out for any points in the dart leg at which you need to pivot the needle slightly, such as on the Megan skirt darts. Backstitching at the tip of the dart can leave a little lump in the dart, so instead stitch off the end of the dart, cut the threads loose, and tie them together by hand into a double knot.

3 The secret to a good-looking dart is pressing. Press horizontal darts downward and vertical darts toward the center. Press on both wrong and right sides of the fabric, using steam if your fabric can take it. A tailor's ham can help create a smooth curve to the fabric, but if you don't have one, a tightly rolled towel will work, too.

See next page for dart tucks.

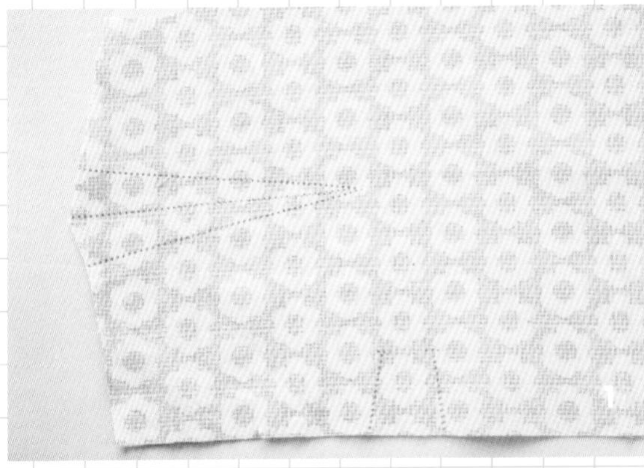
1

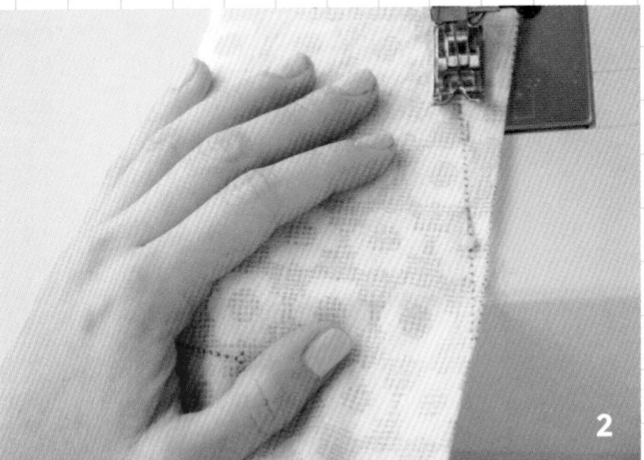
2

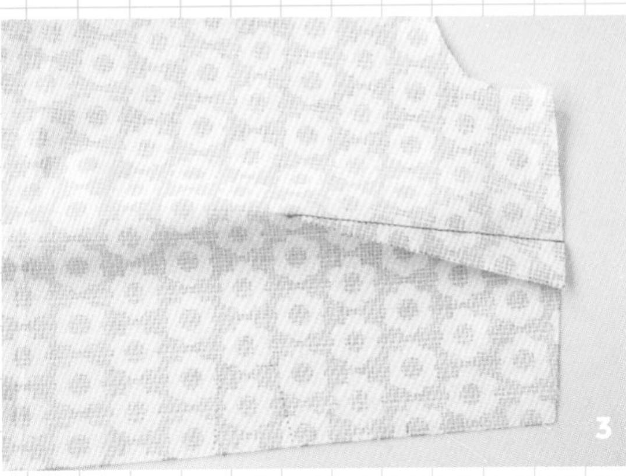
3

TO STITCH A DART TUCK

1 Sew a dart tuck in the same way as a dart, but only stitch to the end of the markings (this time you can backstitch at both ends). The rest of the fold remains unstitched to create a softer shape.

> **PRESSING DARTS**
> Pressing a dart fold can leave a mark on some fabrics. To avoid this, you can slip a slim piece of cardboard between the dart fold and the fabric when pressing.

5 Stitch the front and back bodices together. Pin the pieces, right sides together, at the shoulder seams and stitch. Pin the side seams, right sides together, adjusting the fit if necessary, and stitch those. Finish the shoulder and side seams using zigzag stitch or an overlocker, and press them open or toward the back.

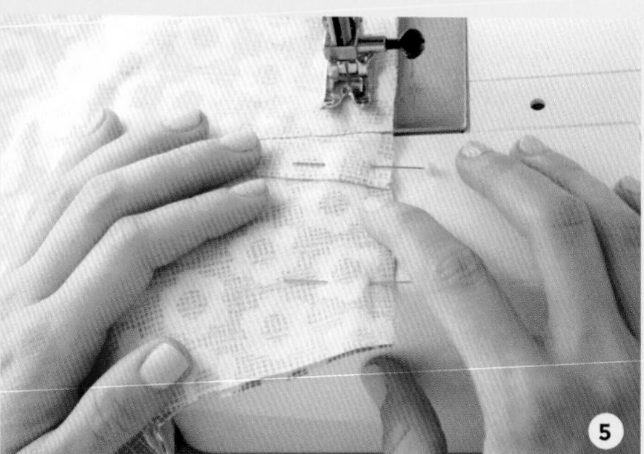

6 Stitch all the darts on the front and back skirt pieces. There are two darts on the front and one dart on each back piece. Press each dart toward the center.

> **MATCHING DARTS**
> If you've moved the vertical tucks and darts on the bodice, move the darts on the skirt, too, so they match up when the bodice and skirt are sewn together.

7 Stitch the front and back skirt pieces together. Pin the front skirt to the back skirt at the side seams, right sides together. Stitch the side seams, then finish the seam allowances and press them either open or toward the back.

8

8 Stitch the bodice and skirt together. Pin the bodice to the skirt, right sides together, matching side seams and waistline darts and dart tucks. Stitch, then finish the seam allowances and press them toward the bodice.

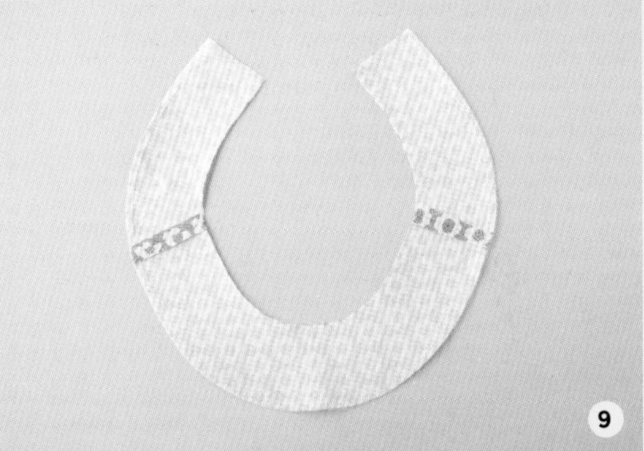

9

9 Construct the neckline facing. Apply the iron-on interfacing to the wrong side of the front and back neckline facings using an iron.

Pin the front and back neckline facings together at the shoulder seams, right sides together, matching notches. Stitch the seams, then trim and press the seam allowances open. (If your fabric is likely to fray, you may want to finish the seams, too.) Finish the outside edge of the facing using zigzag stitch or an overlocker.

10

10 Attach the neckline facing to the bodice. Pin the neckline facing to the bodice neckline, right sides together, matching shoulder seams and center front notches. Stitch the seams and trim the seam allowances. Understitch the facing to the seams, then press the facing to the inside of the dress (see the Attaching a Neckline Facing technique, page 104). If you like, you can secure the neckline facing to the bodice at the shoulder seams with a few stitches, either by hand or by machine stitching in the ditch.

Attaching a Neckline Facing

TECHNIQUE

Facings are used to finish raw edges of a garment that wouldn't otherwise be attached to another seam, such as the waistband on the Delphine Skirt and the neckline on the Megan Dress. A piece of fabric is cut to match the raw edge, sewn to it, then rolled to the inside of the garment to create a neat finish.

1 Pin the facing to the neckline of the bodice, right sides together, aligning the shoulder seams first, then the center front, and finally the rest of the neckline. Stitch along this edge, using a 1⁄16" (1.5 mm) stitch length to help achieve a smooth curve.

2 Trim the seam allowances down closer to the stitching line—one more than the other if your fabric is thick—to reduce bulk. (Remember: you're trimming the seam allowances, not the facing itself.)

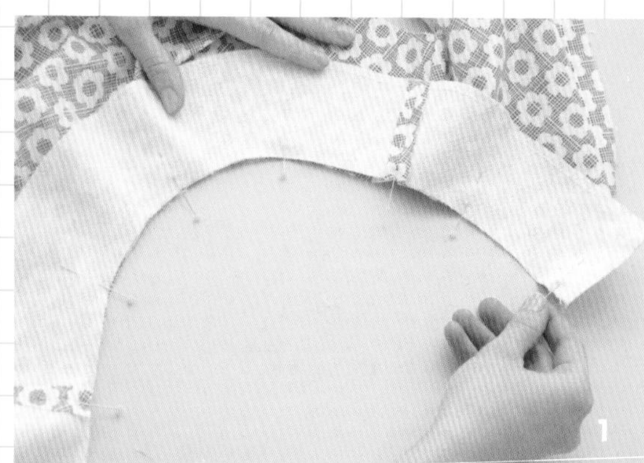
1

MATCHING CURVES
The staystitching should have helped hold the fabric in shape, but occasionally the curves still don't match up exactly: perhaps they weren't quite cut or sewn to the exact same measurements, or the interfacing holds the facing in shape more firmly than the neckline. It's not the end of the world if this happens—you should be able to move one of the raw edges up or down slightly until it matches the other. If they still won't match, lay the pieces flat against each other and trim the larger one down.

CURVED SEAM ALLOWANCES
You can clip a curved seam allowance to create flaps that overlap or spread so the seam allowance will lie flat when it is turned back. These can get a bit messy, so I prefer to just trim the seam allowances close to the stitching line.

3 Press the seam allowances and the facing away from the bodice on both the wrong and right sides. Now we're going to understitch the facing to the seam allowances, which means stitching the facing to the seam allowances

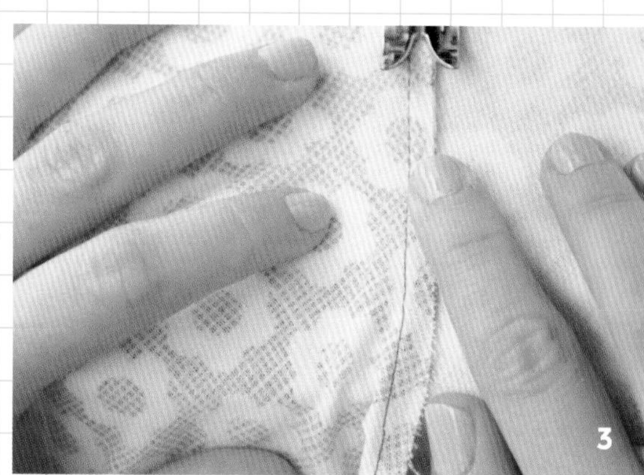
3

close to the seamline to prevent the facing from rolling to the outside of the garment. Do this from the wrong side, so that you can easily see the narrow seam allowance you are stitching along. Hold the fabric taut on each side of the needle while stitching.

4 Turn the facing to the inside of the dress and press it in place. Use some steam from your iron to soften the seamline, then gently roll it 1⁄16" (1.5 mm) or so to the inside of the garment so it's not visible from the outside.

4

⓫ Insert the invisible zipper into the dress back opening. Try on the dress and adjust the back opening seams if need be. Press the seamlines and finish the seam allowances, then insert the zipper, aligning the top of the zipper top stop with the neckline, matching up waistline seams, and keeping the facing folded up and out of the way. Stitch the rest of the skirt seam using a regular zipper foot. Press the seam allowances open.

Open the zipper. Fold the back neckline facings over the back bodice, right sides together, and pin the back opening edge of each facing to the bodice, with the zipper tapes wedged between them (you can trim the top of the zipper tapes down first if you like). Using a regular zipper foot, stitch the edge of the facing down close to the zipper teeth. Fold the seam allowances neatly at the corner and turn the facing right side out. Use a pin to ease the fabric into a point on the right side.

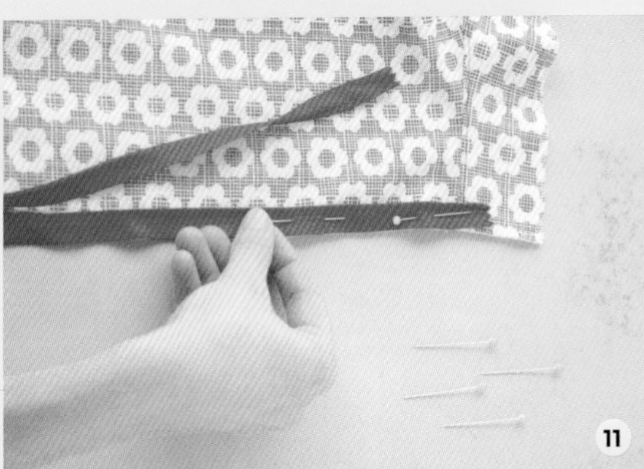

11

⓬ Sew the sleeves and fit them into the bodice. Sew three rows of gathering stitches along the sleeve cap between the gather points (the small circles). Stitch the sleeve underarm seams, then trim and finish the seam allowances and press them either open or toward the back. Turn under a double 5⁄8" (1.5 cm) hem, press, and pin in place. Topstitch close to the upper folded edge.

Pin the sleeves into the armholes, matching underarm seams to bodice side seams, shoulder seams and notches, and pulling on the gathers to fit. Stitch the sleeves in place (see the Setting in Sleeves technique, page 106).

12

SETTING IN SLEEVES

TECHNIQUE

Key skill alert! We're going to add some sleeves to this dress.

1 The top edge of the sleeve—the cap—is usually longer than the armhole that it is being sewn into. Gathering (or easing) the extra fabric into the sleeve allows it to curve over the shoulder. To ease this extra fabric in, you will start by adding gathering stitches to the top edge of the sleeve. Thread your machine in a contrasting color and set the stitch length to 3/16" (4 mm) to sew longer, temporary stitches. Starting about 5/16" (7 mm) away from the raw edge, stitch three rows parallel to each other on the sleeve cap, between the gather points, about 1/4" (5 mm) apart. (For more on gathering, see page 125.)

2 Pin the sleeve underarm seams, right sides together, matching notches. Rethread your machine with matching thread and reset the stitch length to $\frac{1}{16}$–$\frac{1}{8}$" (1.5–3 mm). Stitch the seams, then finish the seam allowances and press them either open or toward the back.

3 Turn the sleeve hem under $\frac{5}{8}$" (1.5 cm) and press. Turn it under another $\frac{5}{8}$" (1.5 cm), press again, and pin in place. Topstitch close to the upper folded edge.

4 Now we're going to align the sleeve and armhole. The way to check you're inserting the correct sleeve into its corresponding armhole is to look at the little notches you cut. The front of the sleeve and armhole have single notches; the backs have double notches. Align the sleeve and armhole, with the fabric right sides together. This can cause a little brain-ache at first, but all you need to do is hold the sleeve right side out and turn the garment on top of it, so the right sides are touching. Then line up the two raw edges of the sleeve and armhole seams.

5 Pin the sleeve and armhole together: this bit is a careful operation. Stick the pins in perpendicular to the edge, on the sleeve side (so the sleeve gathers are facing up when you stitch over them). Rather than sticking the pins in willy-nilly, it's a good idea to pin at strategic points. Pin the underarm seam to match the bodice side seam; pin the sleeve and armhole notches together (those single and double snips mentioned earlier); pin just outside the start and end points of the gather stitches; and pin the shoulder seam to the central point on sleeve.

6 Gently pull on the gathering stitches to bunch up the fabric until the sleeve fits into the armhole. Smooth out the gathers to make them nice and even. Now stick in loads of pins to help keep the gathers even when you stitch over them.

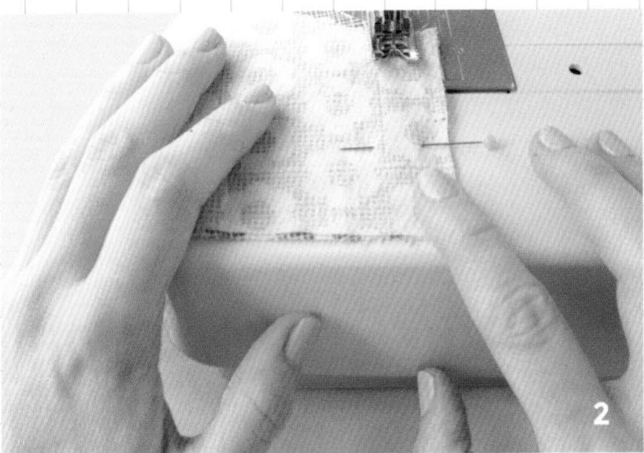
2

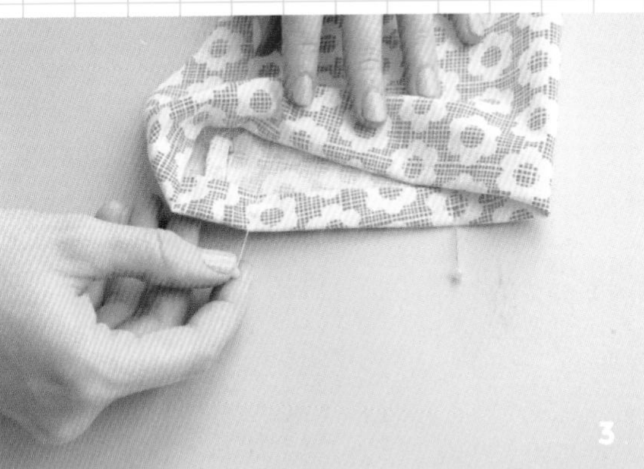
3

5

6

7 If you're confident you can go right ahead and stitch. It's a good idea to machine-baste first though to check you're happy with your gathering. Thread your machine in a contrasting color and set the stitch length to 3⁄16" (4 mm). Stitch just within the seam allowance, about 3⁄8" (1 cm) from the raw edge, starting at the underarm seam. Stitch slowly over the gathers so you can keep them evenly spaced as you go. Sew full circle to meet your starting point.

Once you're happy with your basting, rethread your machine in thread to match your fabric, reset the stitch length to normal—1⁄16–1⁄8" (1.5–3 mm)—and sew your real stitches, overlapping the first stitches with the last to secure them. Now you can remove your basting and gathering stitches with a seam ripper.

8 All that's left to do now is finish your seams and press them. When pressing the armhole, turn the garment inside out and press along the seam. Try not to press the shoulder area, otherwise you'll lose the fullness you've created with your gathers.

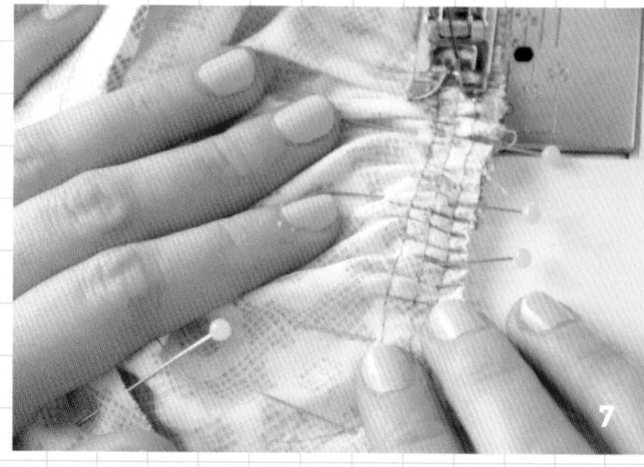

7

Admire your hard work. Hooray! You set in a sleeve! They're not the easiest things in the world to sew, but they do get easier with practice, I promise.

⓭ **Hem the dress.** The Megan Dress includes a 1¼" (3 cm) hem allowance. Try the dress on and adjust the hemline to your preference. Turn under the hem by 5⁄8" (1.5 cm) and press. Turn under another 5⁄8" (1.5 cm), press, and pin. Topstitch the hem in place.

Give everything a final press and fix yourself a well-deserved martini!

13

Warren Chetham-Strode
Three Men and a Girl
Three Men and a Girl
Warren Chetham-Strode
Three Men and a Girl
Chetham-Strode

OLYMPUS TRIP 35

MAKE IT YOUR OWN

CREATE A FAUX PLACKET

Fashion a super-cute faux placket and attach it to the front bodice after stitching the darts and before attaching the facing.

1 Cut a square of contrasting fabric parallel to the selvage, measuring 5" x 5" (13 cm x 13 cm).

2 Apply interfacing to the wrong side of the square. Fold the square in half lengthwise, right sides together, and press. Stitch around one short and the long open edge, pivoting at the corner. Clip the corner, trim the seam allowances, and press them open. Turn the placket right side out and coax the corner of the fabric into a point with a pin. Press.

3 Pin the placket onto the dress, aligning the raw edge with the center front neckline. Topstitch around the placket in matching thread, close to the edge. Sew on decorative buttons by hand.

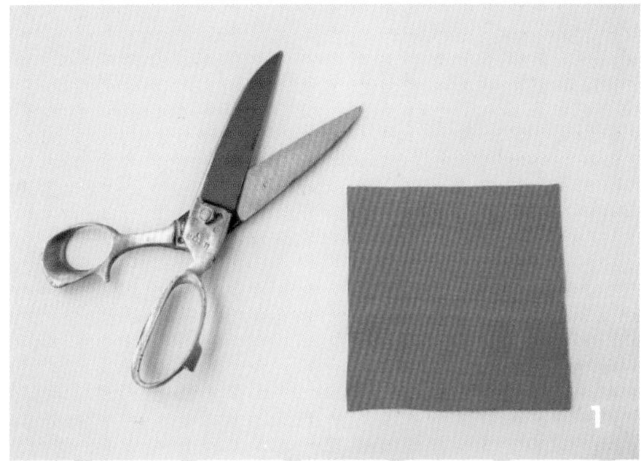
1

2

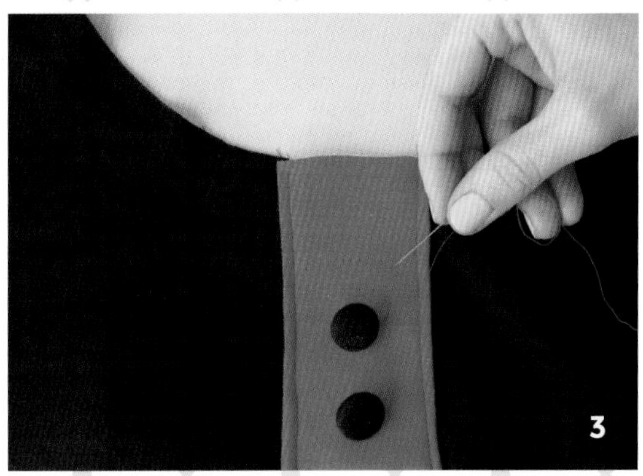
3

ADD A RIBBON TRIM

Create a nautical look by sewing on a ribbon trim at the hemline. I've used ¼" (5 mm) ribbon.

1. Pin the ribbon around the hemline of the dress, starting about ¼" (5 mm) before the center back seam. Stitch along the middle of the ribbon in matching thread, holding both the fabric and ribbon taut to avoid bunching. Once you've come full circle, fold under ¼" (5 mm) of ribbon, covering the starting point, and stitch it down. Press with steam to help "set" the stitches and flatten the ribbon and fabric.
2. Sew on a second length of ribbon ¼" (5 mm) below the first one.

SOME MORE IDEAS...

- ◊ Play around with color blocking—mix and match the sleeves, bodice, skirt, and optional placket in two or more colors.
- ◊ Make a bow and attach it at the waist.
- ◊ Attach a panel of lace in place of the faux placket.
- ◊ Use fancy topstitching on the hemline (page 36).
- ◊ Insert piping along the waistline seam (page 153).

MAKE IT A LIFESTYLE

BECOMING A DESIGNER

For me, being a DIY dressmaker isn't simply about following a pattern or mastering a series of techniques. It's about designing and creating beautiful clothing that is unique to me—clothing made to my own specifications and that I know no one else owns. The spirit of DIY isn't about feeling restricted by a set of instructions or bound to the designer's interpretation of a pattern—it's about being in control. A sewing pattern is a template to get you started, but it's your own creativity that will make the finished product something that you love. So I encourage you to approach a dressmaking project like a blank canvas—you can project your own vision onto it and add extra touches to make it special.

So how do you go about designing a dressmaking project? Not everyone thinks of themselves as creative, so here are some tips on getting started.

First of all, be open to dressmaking inspiration wherever you go. Perhaps you spot a beautiful dress on a stranger in the street, an incredible outfit in an old movie, or an unusual color combination in an artwork. Keeping both a sketchbook of ideas and online pinboard of garments and details you love can provide you with a lifetime of dressmaking inspiration.

When considering sewing patterns, as well as looking at the photos of the designer's version of the finished garment, take a look at the simple line illustration that is usually included (at the beginning of each chapter in this book). This will give you a clear idea of the shape and style lines of the design, without overly influencing your ideas of what fabrics to pair it with. Keeping this line drawing in your head, imagine how it would look in a particular color or palette of colors. Consider prints, too—hold up a fabric swatch and picture what the finished garment would look like, with shoes, accessories and all. You could even trace the line drawing and have some fun coloring in.

As well as colors and prints, think about what embellishments you could add, such as piping, a bow, or fabric-covered buttons. The "Make It Your Own" sections of this book provide you with lots of techniques and ideas for how to add a special touch to any garment. Alternatively, if your style is more about minimalism, you could always remove features from a pattern and keep it simple.

As your understanding of clothing construction grows, you'll be able to alter the pattern pieces themselves, too. Try changing the shape of the collar or lengthening a top into a dress. Some DIY dressmakers have lots of fun creating a "Frankenpattern," in other words, combining the top half from one pattern with the bottom half from a totally different pattern, to end up with something that's hopefully not a monster but a masterpiece!

Now that you can make your own clothes, you no longer need to feel restricted by whatever styles happen to be in the stores at the moment. When it comes to your wardrobe, the sky is the limit, so get designing!

CLÉMENCE SKIRT

CHAPTER 5

With the Clémence Skirt, you'll get a gentle introduction to making your own easy-peasy pattern from scratch. This classic dirndl skirt is composed of rectangular pieces of fabric gathered into a waistband, closing with an invisible zipper at center back. You'll learn the wonders of gathering and finishing with beautiful French seams. Clémence is one of those great "blank canvas" garments that will show off a fabric really well: now's the time to break out those crazy prints!

SUPPLIES

$1\frac{5}{8}$–$2\frac{1}{4}$ yd (1.5–2 m) of fabric, depending on your pattern dimensions

8" (20 cm) invisible zipper (in color to match your fabric)

Iron-on interfacing (in similar weight to your fabric)

Thread (in color to match your fabric)

TOOLS

See page 14

Zipper foot

Invisible zipper foot

Paper to make pattern

Drawing tools, including long ruler and drafting triangle (or something with a 90-degree angle)

OPTIONAL

39" x 12" (100 cm x 30 cm) of fabric and small amount of iron-on interfacing, for pockets (page 130)

½ yd (50 cm) of extra fabric and iron-on interfacing, and two hooks and eyes, for the bow belt (page 133)

TECHNIQUES

Setting up your sewing machine (page 21)
Stitching school (page 26)
Pinning (page 30)
Adjusting stitches (page 32)
Choosing your fabric (page 44)
Laying out fabric and pattern (page 48)
Cutting out fabric pieces (page 50)
Understanding clothing construction (page 54)
Pressing matters (page 57)
Hemming (page 60)
Interfacing (page 77)
Inserting an invisible zipper (page 80)
Making a simple skirt pattern (page 120)
French seams (page 123)
Gathering (page 125)
Stitch in the ditch (page 128)

FABRIC SUGGESTIONS

Choose a medium-weight cotton (including chambray, poplin, and quilting cottons), a lightweight linen, or something a bit more posh, such as silk shantung. Alternatively, a lightweight cotton lawn will give your skirt a more floaty silhouette. Avoid anything too heavy or the gathering may prove tricky. This skirt looks great in both solid colors and prints—polka dots, bicycles, nautical scenes, kittens, you name it!

TO MAKE THE SKIRT

❶ **Draft your skirt pattern.** Draft your paper pattern pieces to your waist measurement and desired fullness and hem length (see the Making a Simple Skirt Pattern technique, below).

MAKING A SIMPLE SKIRT PATTERN

TECHNIQUE

This must be one of the easiest patterns in the world to make—nothing scary here, I promise. We're going to make the skirt twice the measurement of our hips to create some lovely fullness, gathering it into a fitted waistband. I'll let you in on a little secret—the only part you need to be accurate about measuring correctly is the waistband. If you alter the measurements of the rest of the skirt a little bit, it's not going to mess anything up. You can always increase or decrease the width of the skirt if you want to vary the fullness, for example.

To begin, note down measurements for your waist, your hips, and from your waist to the point where you'd like the hemline to fall. I like mine to land just above the knee, but pick a hemline to suit your style.

Next, calculate and note down the following measurements for your pattern pieces.

FRONT SKIRT PATTERN PIECE

WIDTH: Half of your hip measurement, plus ⅝" (1.5 cm) for seam allowance.

(For example, if your hips are 39"/100 cm, the width of your front skirt piece will be 20⅛"/51.5 cm.)

LENGTH: Waist to hemline measurement, plus ⅝" (1.5 cm) top seam allowance, plus 1¼" (3 cm) hem allowance.

(For example, for a finished skirt that's 20"/50 cm long, the length of your front skirt piece will be 21⅞"/54.5 cm.)

BACK SKIRT PATTERN PIECE

WIDTH: Half of your hip measurement, plus 2 x ⅝" (1.5 cm) seam allowances.

(For example, if your hips are 39"/100 cm, the width of your back skirt will be 20¾"/53 cm.)

LENGTH: Same as front skirt.

WAISTBAND PATTERN PIECE

LENGTH: Half of your waist measurement, plus ⅝" (1.5 cm) seam allowance, plus ⅝" (1.5 cm) ease.

(For example, if your waist is 31½"/80 cm, the width of your waistband will be 17"/43 cm.)

WIDTH: 2¼" (6 cm), plus 2 x ⅝" (1.5 cm) seam allowances = 3½" (9 cm).

DRAWING THE PATTERN PIECES

Draw out these three rectangles on some paper, using a long ruler and making sure your corners are 90-degree angles. You don't need to get any special kind of paper to make patterns. Try flipchart paper (nice and large), kitchen baking paper (great for tracing), parcel paper (less susceptible to ripping)—whatever you want really.

Now to add in the pattern details so you know what these pieces of paper are when you pull them out again at a later date. Label the pattern pieces with the following information.

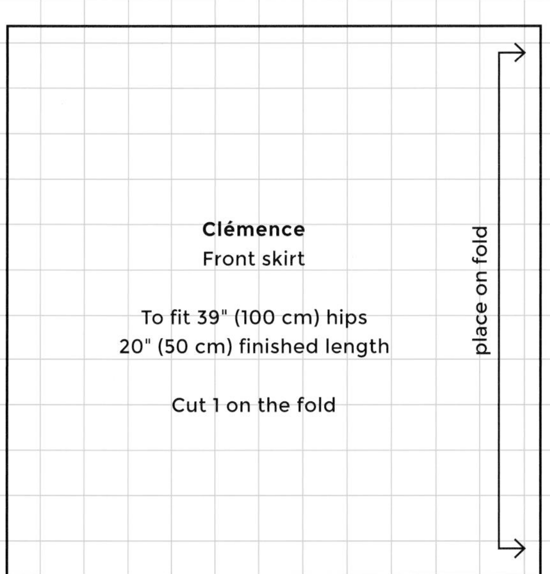

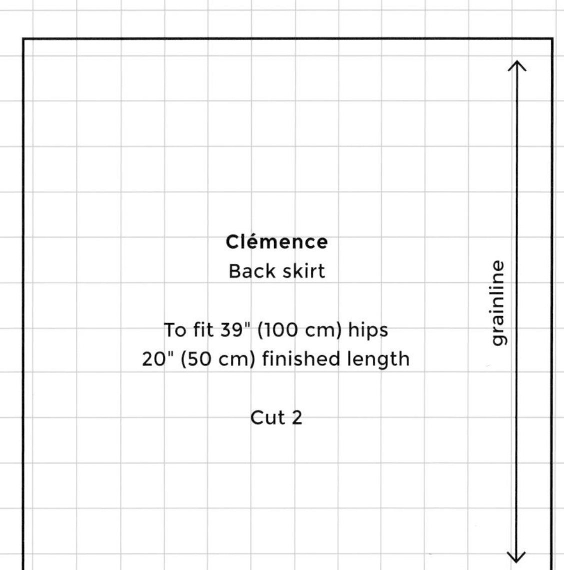

Clémence Waistband
To fit 31½" (80 cm) waist

Cut 2 on the fold
+ 1 interfacing

place on fold

And you've made a pattern—woop!

MEASURING YOUR WAIST

When measuring your waist, choose the point at which you'd like the waistband of your skirt to sit—whether your preference is high or low.

❷ **Cut out your fabric skirt pieces.** Pin the paper pattern pieces to the fabric and cut two back skirts, one front skirt on the fold, and two waistbands on the fold. Cut one interfacing waistband on the fold. Notch the seam allowances at the center top of the front skirt and center bottom of the waistbands.

❸ **Interface the waistband piece.** Apply iron-on interfacing to one of the waistband pieces. This will be the waistband (the piece that shows on the outside of the skirt); the other piece will be the waistband facing (on the inside of the skirt).

❹ **Stitch the skirt side seams.** Using French seams, stitch the side seams (see the French Seams technique, opposite).

FABRIC WIDTH

If your fabric is too narrow for your pattern, you could rotate the skirt pieces as if the grainline were horizontal, as long as that doesn't mess up directional prints. If you do this, let your skirt hang for a day before hemming in case it stretches.

FRENCH SEAMS

TECHNIQUE

This skirt is a great opportunity to introduce you to some good friends of mine, French seams—known as "English seams" to the French, curiously enough!

French seams enclose the raw edges of the fabric, creating a lovely, neat finish to your garment. They work really nicely on lightweight to medium-weight fabric, but not so great on heavier fabrics. They're particularly useful on sheer fabrics as they are less conspicuous than overlocked seams, and the strength of the seam makes them practical for clothing that's going to go through the laundry a lot.

You know how you usually sew fabric right sides together? Well, with French seams you start by stitching the fabric wrong sides together. *Sacré bleu!* Intrigued? Let's go . . .

1

1 Pin the front skirt and back skirt pieces at the side seams, wrong sides together. Stitch using a ¼" (5 mm) seam allowance, backstitching at each end. Trim any pesky fraying edges. If sewing such a narrow seam allowance worries you, stitch it a little wider then trim it down.

2 Press the seams flat to help "set" the stitches, then press the seams open on both wrong and right sides.

2

3 Fold the fabric right sides together along the stitching line and press along the fold. Pin along the seam.

4 Stitch the seams right sides together with a ⅜" (1 cm) seam allowance, backstitching at each end. The raw edges should now be hidden away within the two lines of stitching.

5 Press the seams toward the back.

Now admire your handiwork—*très joli!*

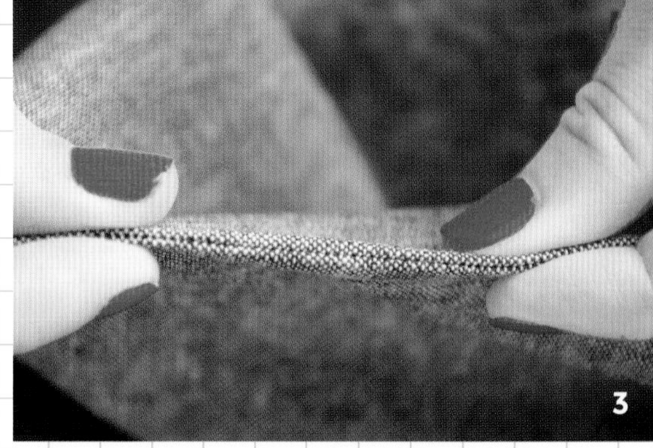
3

4

5

❺ Gather the top edge of the skirt to fit the waistband. Using a contrasting thread, sew three rows of gathering stitches along the top edge of the skirt.

Right sides together, pin the center notches in the lower edge of the (interfaced) waistband and the top of the skirt together. Pull up the gathers until the skirt fits the waistband, then pin and baste the pieces together. Using thread that matches the color of your fabric, stitch the pieces together, then remove the gathering and basting stitches (see the Gathering technique, opposite).

5

GATHERING

TECHNIQUE

Gathering creates fullness in an area of a garment, such as a waistline or sleeve cap. You sew long, temporary stitches across the area, then pull the stitches to gather the fabric. The first couple of times your gathers may not turn out perfectly even, but who's going to notice?

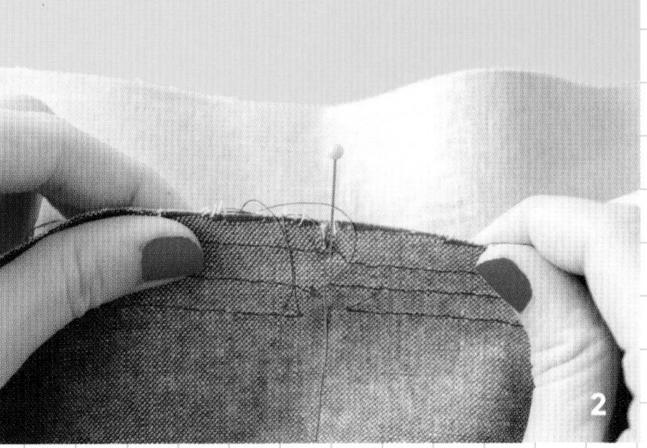

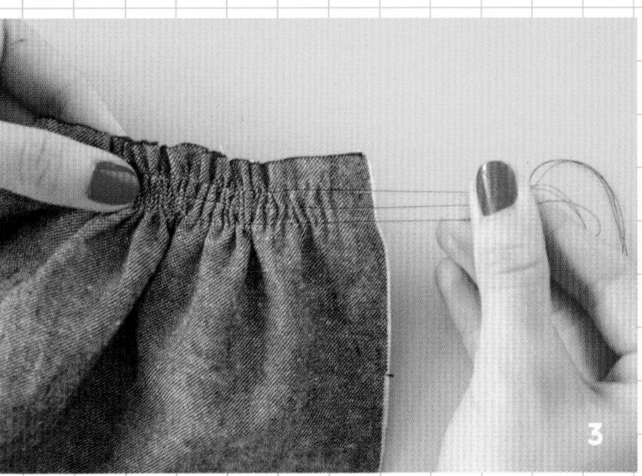

1 Thread your machine in a contrasting color—this will make it easy to see the stitches when you pull them out later. Set your stitch length to 3⁄16" (4 mm) and turn the thread tension dial to a lower setting to create long stitches that you can pull on.

Sew three rows of long stitches parallel to each other, about ¼" (5 mm) apart, along the edge to be gathered. It'll help if two of your rows can straddle the ⅝" (1.5 cm) seamline, but try to avoid sewing a row directly on top of this line so your "real" stitches aren't on top of the gathering—I do mine at about ¼" (5 mm), ½" (12 mm), and ¾" (17 mm) from the edge.

Gathering too much fabric at once can cause the threads to snap, so on a long area such as the top of the Clémence Skirt, divide the area into segments to gather separately: from one back opening to one side seam, side seam to center front, center front to the other side seam, side seam to back opening. Be careful to avoid stitching over the French seams. Don't backstitch at each end; instead, leave a length of thread at each end so you have something to pull on. Reset the thread tension correctly now, before you forget.

2 Now you're ready to begin joining the gathered edge to the piece it is to be sewn to. Pin the (interfaced) waistband and the top of the skirt right sides together at the center front notches—starting like this will help ensure the gathering ends up symmetrical.

3 Take hold of the set of three thread tails that come from the bobbin (you'll find them easier

to pull than the spool tails) and gently pull on them to bunch up the fabric, smoothing the gathers along with your fingers. I like to pull halfway along from one end and halfway from the other end of each segment of gathers to avoid the threads pulling out of the fabric completely. Gather the fabric until it fits the edge it is to be sewn to—in the case of the Clémence Skirt, it needs to fit the long edge of the waistband.

4 Smooth out the gathers so they're evenly distributed all the way along the fabric. Pin the waistband in place right along the gathered edge using plenty of pins.

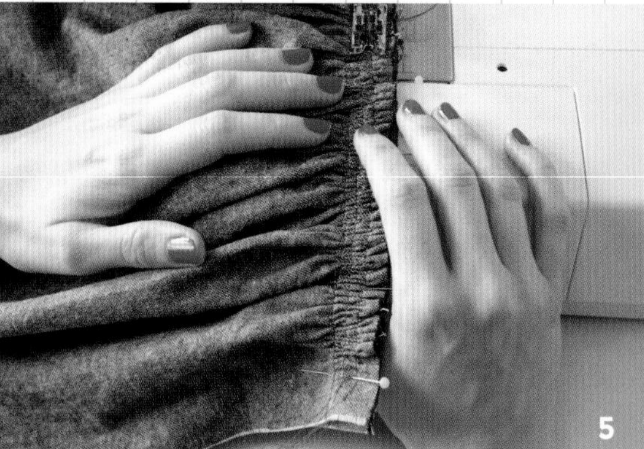

5 Machine-baste across the gathers, stitching with a ⅜" (1 cm) seam allowance. Sew with the gathers facing up so you can keep them smooth while stitching (mind your fingers!). Once you're happy with your basting, rethread your machine with a thread that matches the color of your fabric, reset the stitch length to ¹⁄₁₆–⅛" (1.5–3 mm), and stitch across the gathers. Remove the gathering and basting stitches.

(NOT) IRONING GATHERS
Be careful not to press over gathers, or they will lose their lovely fullness. Use the tip of your iron to press the seam without squishing the gathers.

❻ **Trim the skirt waistband seams.** Press the waistband and seam allowances up and away from the skirt.

❼ Insert the invisible zipper into the center back of the skirt. Place the top stop of the zipper ⅝" (1.5 cm) down from the top of the waistband and sew in place. Pin the rest of the center back seam together and stitch using a regular zipper foot. Press the seam allowances open.

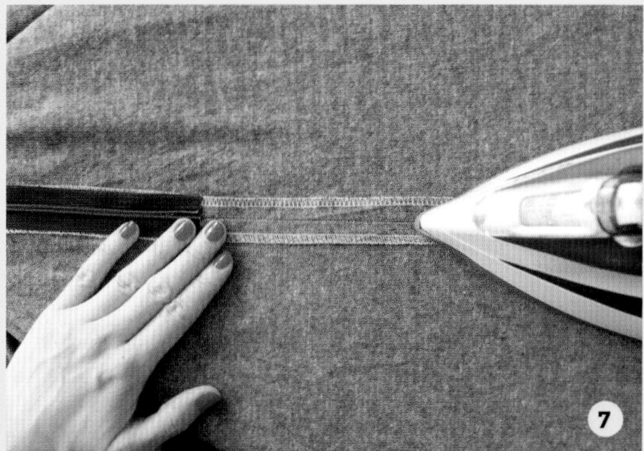
7

❽ Attach the facing to the waistband. Press under ⅜" (1 cm) along the bottom edge of the facing, wrong sides together. The reason we're only pressing under ⅜" (1 cm), not ⅝" (1.5 cm), is to make it easier to "stitch in the ditch" later on.

Open the zipper, then pin and stitch the waistband to the facing, following Step 9 of Delphine Skirt (page 83). Trim the seam allowances to about half their width.

8

❾ Turn the waistband to the right side. Fold the corners neatly then turn the waistband right side out (Step 11, page 83). Tease out the corner from the right side using a pin. Press the waistband, rolling the seam slightly toward the inside of the garment so it's not visible from the outside.

9

❿ Stitch the waistband in place. From the right side of the skirt, pin the bottom edge of the facing to the inside of the skirt, making sure the fold covers the seamline. Stitch in the ditch to sew the facing to the skirt (see the Stitch in the Ditch technique, page 128). Alternatively, you could topstitch or slipstitch (page 173) the facing down.

10

STITCH IN THE DITCH

TECHNIQUE

Stitching in the ditch basically means machine stitching on top of an existing seamline—the "ditch"—so you can't see the stitches from the outside of the garment.

1 The way I check that the stitching is going to catch the facing on the other side is to pin exactly along the line that I'm going to stitch; pin along the seamline from the right side of the skirt. Then look at the inside of the skirt and check that the pins are holding down the facing all the way along. If they're not, adjust the fold, press, and repin as needed.

1

2 Carefully stitch from the right side, exactly along the seamline. I like to make the challenge of stitching exactly within the ditch a bit of a game, but don't worry if it doesn't turn out perfect and some stitches go off piste—for I do believe life's too short to stress out over the little things.

2

⓫ **Hem the skirt.** When you made the pattern (yes, you!), you included a 1¼" (3 cm) hem allowance. Fold the hem under by ⅝" (1.5 cm) and press. Fold under by another ⅝" (1.5 cm), press, and pin. Try the skirt on and adjust the hemline if you prefer. Topstitch the hem in place, close to the inside fold.

And admire your handiwork!

11

MAKE IT
YOURSELF

MAKE IT
YOUR OWN

MAKE IT
AGAIN

(AND AGAIN!)

MAKE IT YOUR OWN

SIDE-SEAM POCKETS

Adding pockets to this skirt will make it oh-so practical. You could even make your pockets in a contrasting fabric, just to mix things up a little. Attach the pockets before you stitch the skirt side seams together. To make things easier, we're going to leave out the French seams this time and use another kind of seam finish.

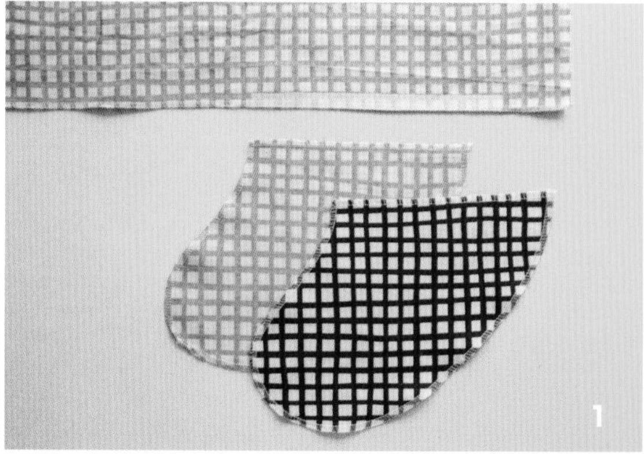

1

1 Cut four of the pocket pattern pieces included in this book. Cut four strips of iron-on interfacing ¾" (2 cm) wide and ¾" (2 cm) longer than the mouth of the pocket (the straight edge). Apply the interfacing to the skirt side seams, with the top of the strip 2" (5 cm) down from the top of the skirt. This will help reinforce the pocket openings. Finish the skirt side seams using zigzag stitch or an overlocker. Finish the edges of all four pocket pieces in the same way.

2

2 Pin the mouth of one pocket piece to each skirt side seam, right sides together, placing the top of the pocket 2½" (6 cm) down from the top edge of the skirt. Using a ⅜" (1 cm) seam allowance, stitch the pocket mouth to the skirt side seam. Fold the pocket away from the skirt so it's sticking out at the side and press along the seamline.

> **REINFORCED POCKETS**
> I like to reinforce the points where the pockets meet the side seams with a few extra stitches to avoid holes forming.

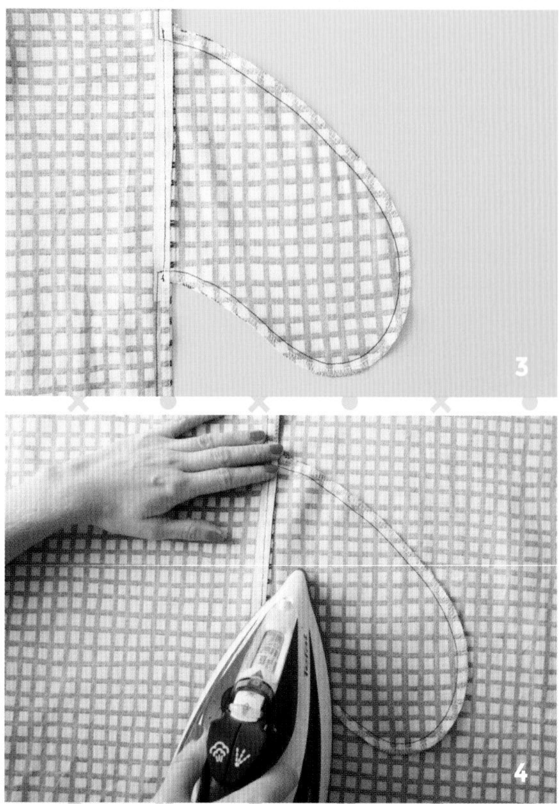

3 Place the skirt front piece against the skirt back pieces, right sides together, matching pockets and side seams. Pin and stitch the side seams and pockets. Starting at the top of the skirt, stitch until the needle reaches the first small circle marking, pivot and stitch around the edge of the pocket to the second small circle, then pivot and stitch down the rest of the skirt side seam. Repeat on the other side seam.

4 Press the pockets and seams toward the front of the skirt.

Make the rest of the skirt, and put your hands in your pockets! Lovely stuff!

BOW BELT

This bow belt will add a gorgeous finishing touch to your Clémence Skirt, Lilou Dress, and more. Make it in matching or contrasting fabric—it's a great way to use up leftover material. For your belt, draw the pattern pieces on some paper to the following measurements.

Belt: length is half of your waist size, plus 2" (5 cm) (cut on fold), by width of 4⅜" (11 cm).

Bow: 12" x 4¾" (30 cm x 12 cm).

Knot: 3" x 3" (8 cm x 8 cm).

1 Cut out one of each piece in your fabric, cutting your belt on the fold so it ends up double the length. Cut iron-on interfacing to the length and half the width of the belt pattern, and apply it to the wrong side of the top half of the belt.

2 Fold the belt in half lengthwise, right sides together, and press. Pin, then stitch along the long side and one of the short sides, leaving one short side unsewn. Snip the corner, then trim the seams and press them open.

1

2

3 Turn the belt right side out so the interfacing is on the inside. I find a chopstick (or similar) helps here. Hold the smooth end of the chopstick against the stitched short end of the belt, then gradually smooth the wrong side of the belt over it. It'll bunch up more and more, and feel like a bit of a chore for a while, but eventually you'll see the end of the belt emerge out of the top of the tube. Grab this end, discard the stick, and gently pull it through (don't yank it too hard!) so the belt turns right side out.

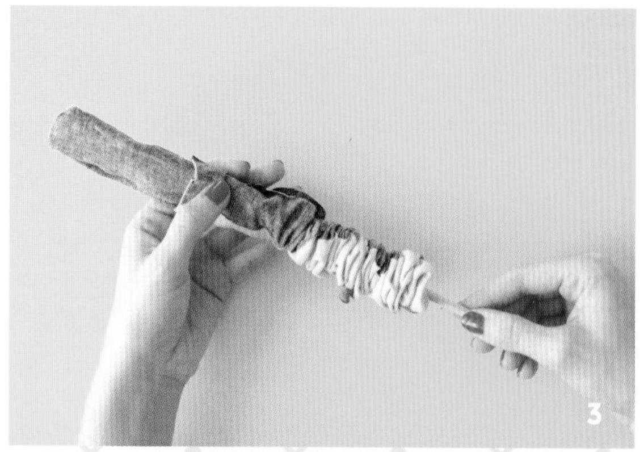
3

4 Right now the belt looks a little like a deflated snake. Let's sharpen it up. First you need to make the corners look a bit more like corners—use a pin to gently coax out the point. Now give the belt a good press, rolling the seamline a tiny bit to the noninterfaced side of the belt. Fold the seam allowance of the unsewn edge inside the belt, and either topstitch or slipstitch (page 173) the end closed.

4

5 Fold the bow in half lengthwise, right sides together, and stitch along the long edge. Trim the seams and press them open. Turn the bow right side out and press, with the seamline in the center of the piece. Place the short ends of the bow together and topstitch them together to form a loop (the ends won't be on show). Position these topstitched ends in the center of the loop and press the bow flat.

Make the knot in the same way, but don't stitch the ends together.

5

6 Pinch the center of the bow into a concertina shape. Wrap the knot tightly around the bow and pin the ends of the knot together to hold the bow in place. Sew the ends of the knot together, either by machine or hand, trimming off any excess fabric if need be.

6

7 Hand sew the bow onto the front of the right-hand end of the belt, catching the bow and knot pieces with the stitches. Hand-sew two hooks onto the underside of the right-hand end of the belt. Try the belt on, mark the positions for the corresponding eyes on the front of the left-hand end, then hand sew them on.

7

Beautiful!

SOME MORE IDEAS...

- ◊ Finish the hem with fancy topstitching in a contrasting color (page 36).
- ◊ Play around with the length of the skirt—try mini, midi, or maxi.
- ◊ Appliqué or hand embroider a design onto the hem of the skirt.
- ◊ Add a ribbon trimming (page 112).
- ◊ Sew patch pockets onto the front of the skirt (page 61).

FITTING SEWING INTO A BUSY LIFE

One of the most common reasons I hear people cite for not sewing is that they don't have time. I know how that feels; I sometimes catch myself making a similar excuse. We're all so busy working, looking after the kids, spending time with friends, sticking to our yoga practice, cleaning the house, handling paperwork, catching up with social media . . . Phew! Just thinking about it is exhausting.

But step back from your to-do list and daily routine for a moment: it should be you who decides how you want to use your time. Often you need to actively make time to do things that you want to do. Even just a few minutes of creativity squeezed into your day can make a huge difference to your happiness.

So here are some tried and tested top tips on fitting sewing into a busy life.

SEW IN SPURTS

Try sewing in short bursts—even if it's just 15 minutes before you go to work or while dinner is in the oven. Slow and steady wins the race—before you know it, you'll have a new dress.

BREAK IT DOWN

If after a long day at work a whole sewing project seems overwhelming, break it down into individual steps and it's much more manageable. Sewing in spurts, you could insert a zipper, stitch a few seams, or prepare facings.

KNOW WHAT COMES NEXT

When you get up from your sewing table, make a note of the next step that you need to do while it's clear in your head. That way, it'll be soooo much easier to get back into the project quickly.

PREPARE YOUR MATERIALS

Before you embark on a new project, prewash your fabric and gather all the stuff you'll need to avoid the frustration of having to stop sewing to go shopping. I keep all the ingredients for a project (thread, interfacing, zippers, buttons, and so on) together in a bag so I know where everything is.

ESTABLISH YOUR SPACE

Being able to leave out your sewing machine and project will save you time setting up and clearing away. Just a table in the corner of a room will make a big difference. If this isn't an option, keep your regular sewing tools (scissors, tape measure, pins) in a box so you can whip them out easily.

DUMP THE DULL PROJECTS

If you've totally lost interest in a project, ditch it. Why bother making something you're not enjoying? Try a quick, easy, and fun project instead, and your sewing mojo will return in a flash.

TAKE A SEWING HOLIDAY

Finally, sewing in short bursts is great, but you can't beat an indulgently long sewing session. Block out the occasional whole day or long weekend to spend at home making dresses. Bliss.

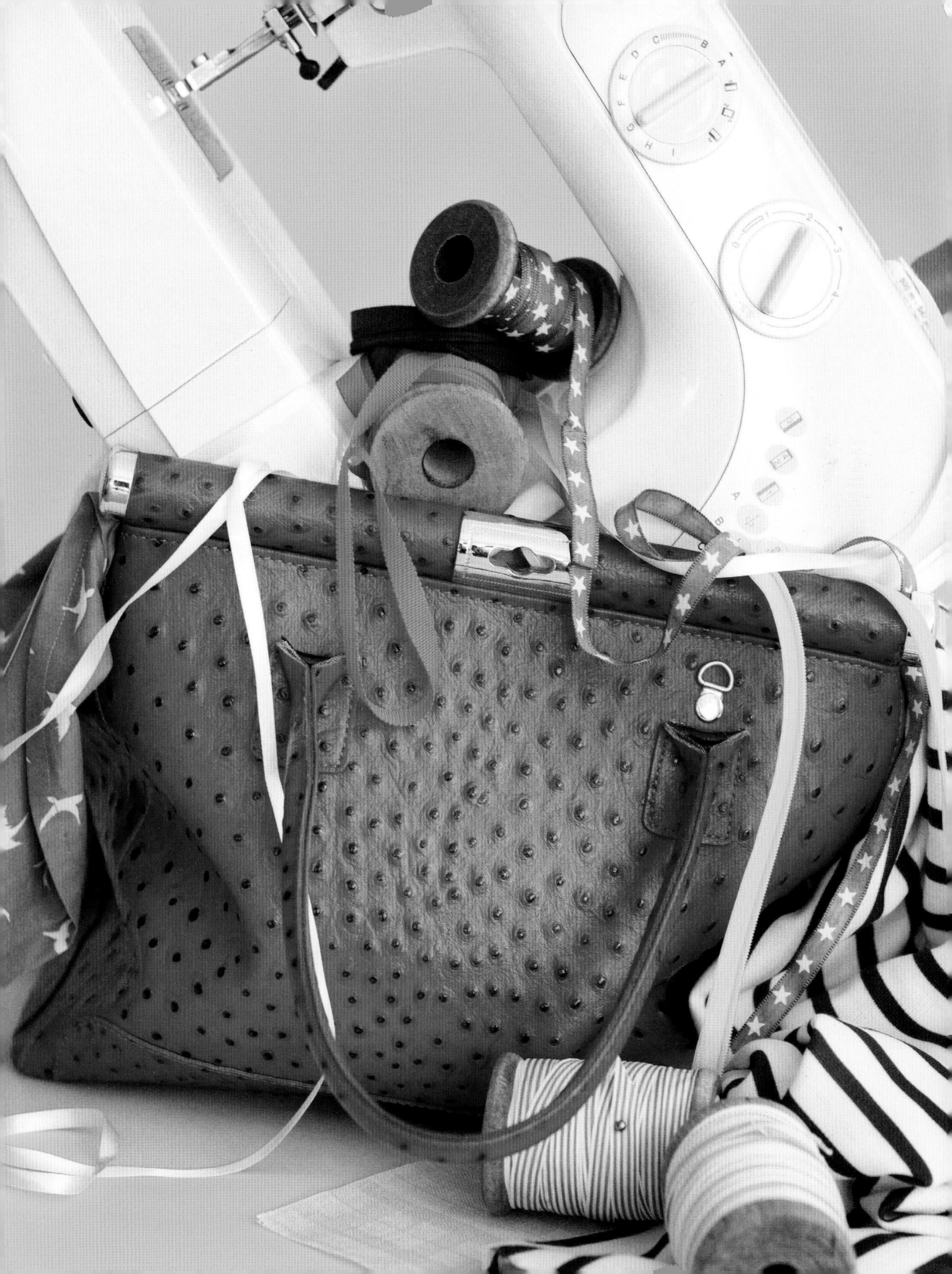

MIMI BLOUSE

CHAPTER 6

Take your skills up a notch with the super-cute Mimi Blouse. If you've followed the techniques in the book up to here, you can handle this project; and it'll definitely take you beyond the status of beginner. The bodice of this loose-fitting, button-up blouse is gathered into a yoke at front and back, with pretty pleated sleeves and a stunning Chelsea collar. Wear it tucked into a skirt for the office or loose over skinny jeans at the weekend.

SUPPLIES

2¼ yd (2 m) length of fabric, 60" (150 cm) wide

OR 2⅝ yd (2.4 m) length of fabric, 45" (115 cm) wide

6 x ½" (12 mm) buttons

Iron-on interfacing (in similar weight to your fabric)

Thread (in color to match your fabric)

TOOLS

See page 14

Buttonhole foot

OPTIONAL

Piping (page 152)

Self-cover buttons and matching or contrasting fabric (page 154)

TECHNIQUES

Setting up your sewing machine (page 21)

Stitching school (page 26)

Pinning (page 30)

Adjusting stitches (page 32)

Choosing your fabric (page 44)

Preparing your pattern (page 47)

Laying out fabric and pattern (page 48)

Cutting out fabric pieces (page 50)

Transferring the markings (page 52)

Understanding clothing construction (page 54)

Simple seam allowance finishes (page 55)

Pressing matters (page 57)

Hemming (page 60)

Pattern sizing (page 72)

Understanding ease (page 75)

Interfacing (page 77)

Fitting your garment (page 96)

Staystitching (page 99)

Attaching a neckline facing (page 104)

Setting in sleeves (page 106)

French seams (page 123)

Gathering (page 125)

Stitch in the ditch (page 128)

Making a collar (page 145)

Buttonholes (page 149)

Sewing on buttons (page 151)

FABRIC SUGGESTIONS

Drape is key here; otherwise the blouse will look stiff. Try a lightweight cotton, such as a lawn or voile, or a lightweight silk, polyester, or blend.

PATTERN DETAILS

The paper pattern has 8 pieces:
Front bodice—cut 2
Back bodice—cut 1 on the fold
Yoke—cut 1 on the fold
Collar—cut 2 on the fold + 1 interfacing
Front facing—cut 2 + 2 interfacing
Neckline facing—cut 1 on the fold + 1 interfacing
Sleeve—cut 2
Sleeve facing—cut 2 + 2 interfacing

Seam allowance is ⅝" (1.5 cm).

PATTERN SIZING

BODY MEASUREMENTS

SIZE	BUST	WAIST	HIP
1	30" (76 cm)	24" (61 cm)	33" (84 cm)
2	32" (81 cm)	26" (66 cm)	35" (89 cm)
3	34" (86.5 cm)	28" (71 cm)	37" (94 cm)
4	36" (91.5 cm)	30" (76 cm)	39" (99 cm)
5	38" (96.5 cm)	32" (81 cm)	41" (104 cm)
6	40" (101.5 cm)	34" (86.5 cm)	43" (109 cm)
7	42" (106.5 cm)	36" (91.5 cm)	45" (114 cm)
8	44" (112 cm)	38" (96.5 cm)	47" (119.5 cm)

FINISHED GARMENT MEASUREMENTS

SIZE	BUST	WAIST	HIP
1	37" (94 cm)	34" (86.5 cm)	39½" (101 cm)
2	39" (99 cm)	36" (91.5 cm)	41½" (106 cm)
3	41" (104 cm)	38" (96.5 cm)	43½" (111 cm)
4	43" (109 cm)	40" (101.5 cm)	45½" (116 cm)
5	45" (114 cm)	42" (106.5 cm)	47½" (121 cm)
6	47" (119.5 cm)	44" (112 cm)	49½" (126 cm)
7	49" (124 cm)	46" (117 cm)	51½" (131 cm)
8	51" (129 cm)	48" (122 cm)	53½" (136 cm)

FABRIC LAYOUT

Here is the suggested arrangement of the pattern pieces on the fabric.

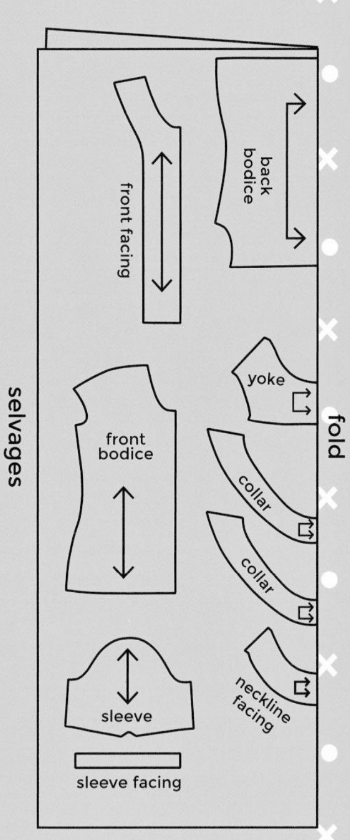

60" (150 cm) wide fabric

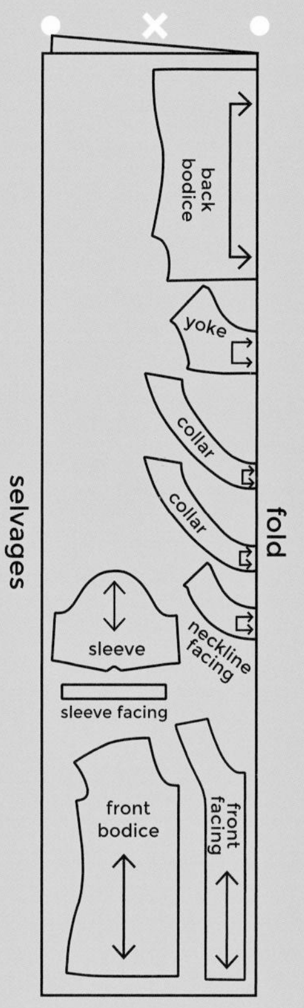

45" (115 cm) wide fabric

TO MAKE THE BLOUSE

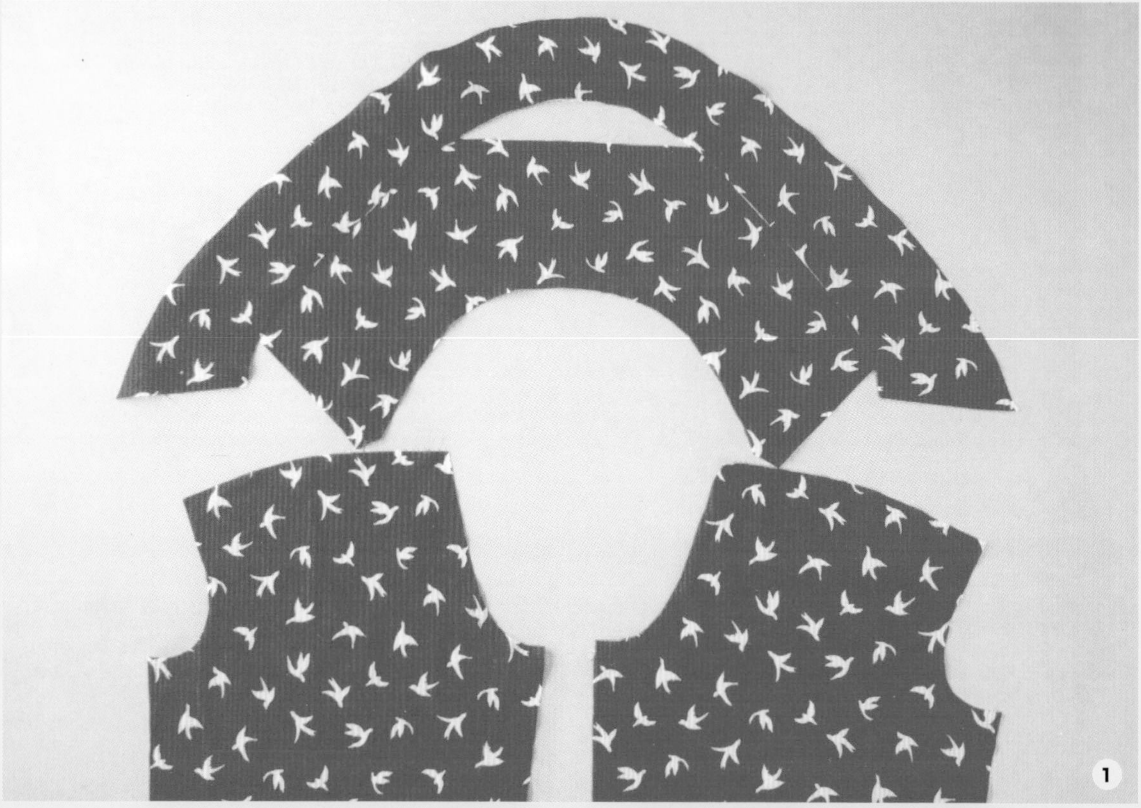

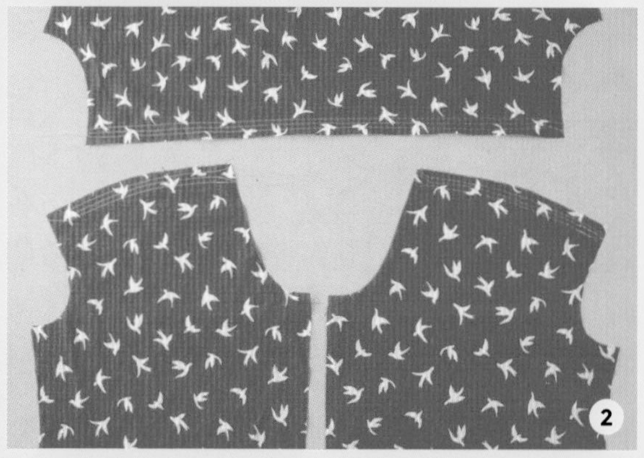

❶ **Cut out your fabric pieces.** Cut out the fabric and interfacing and transfer the pattern markings, including marking the buttonholes on the right side of the fabric on the right front bodice.

Staystitch the neckline on the yoke, front bodice, and collar pieces.

❷ **Sew gathering stitches along the top edge of the front and back bodice pieces.** Thread your machine in a contrasting color and set the stitch length to 3⁄16" (4 mm). Sew three rows of gathering stitches between the small circles on the top edge of each front bodice piece and the back bodice piece.

❸ Gather the bodice edges to fit the yoke, then sew the pieces together. On the back bodice, pull on the gathers to fit the back edge of the yoke. Place the back bodice and yoke right sides together, matching notches, smooth out the gathers, and pin in place. With the gathers facing up on your machine, machine-baste the seams together. Repeat on the front bodice pieces, pulling the gathers up to fit the front edges of the yoke. Once you're happy with the evenness of your basted gathers, rethread your machine in a matching thread, reset the stitch length to 1⁄16–1⁄8" (1.5–3 mm), and stitch the front and back bodice seams to the yoke for real. Remove the gathering and basting stitches. Trim and finish the seams using zigzag stitch or an overlocker. Using the tip of your iron, press the seam allowances toward the yoke, being careful to avoid pressing the gathers.

❹ Now join the front and back bodice together at the side seams. If you want to use French seams, as I did, start by stitching the wrong sides together, using a 1⁄4" (5 mm) seam allowance. Press the seam allowances open and then press the fabric around the seam allowance right sides together. Finally, stitch the seam with a 3⁄8" (1 cm) seam allowance.

Alternatively, you may want to stitch the seam the standard way, right sides together, finishing the seam allowances using zigzag stitch or an overlocker. Now press the seam allowances toward the back.

❺ **Make the collar.** The Mimi Blouse has a Chelsea collar—a delightful shape that looks chic without being too girly. It sits almost flat against the blouse, with some subtle shaping giving it a very slight stand. The flat collar is very easy to adapt; using this one as a starting point, you could experiment with changing the outer edge to make a Peter Pan collar, a scalloped collar, or even just a simple square shape (see the Making a Collar technique, opposite).

❻ **Attach the collar to the bodice.** Align the inner edge of the collar with the bodice neckline, the undercollar against the right side of the bodice, matching notches and aligning the top of the short ends of the collar with the fitting line on the center front of the bodice. Pin in place. Stitch the collar to the bodice neckline using a ⅜" (1 cm) seam allowance. Don't worry about those raw seam allowances on show—we're going to hide those with a facing.

❼ **Construct the facing.** Apply iron-on interfacing to the front facings and neckline facing, using the iron. Place the top edges of the front facings against the bottom edges of the neckline facing, right sides together, and pin. Stitch the seams. Trim the seam allowances to about half their width and press them upward.

Press under about ¼" (5 mm) all around the outer edge of the facing (you don't need to finish the edge as the interfacing will prevent it from fraying). Topstitch the hem and press it.

❽ **Attach the facing to the bodice.** Align the facing with the bodice neckline and center front openings, right sides together and matching notches, with the collar sandwiched between them. Pin in place. With the facing on top, stitch the facing to the bodice, starting at the bottom of one center front opening, stitching around the neckline and down the other center front opening. Be careful to hold the main part of the collar flat so it doesn't get caught in the stitching.

MAKING A COLLAR

TECHNIQUE

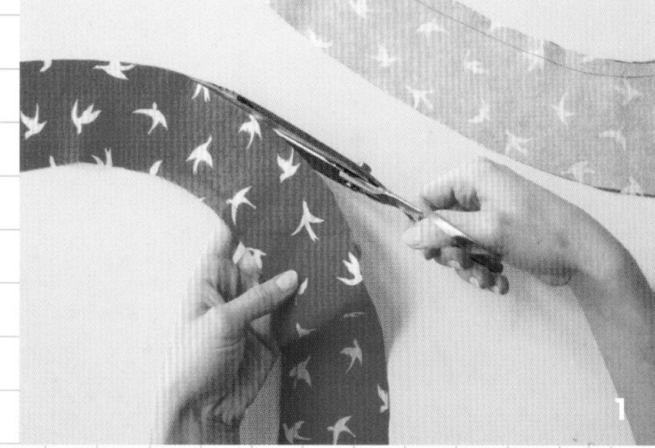

1 Apply iron-on interfacing to one collar piece with the iron: this will be the top collar. The other collar piece will be the undercollar. Trim the short ends and outer edge of the undercollar by ⅛" (3 mm), tapering to no trimming at the inner corner. Do not trim the neckline edge of the undercollar.

TRIMMING THE UNDERCOLLAR
Trimming the undercollar slightly smaller than the collar will encourage the seam to roll to the underside, so you don't see it on the right side.

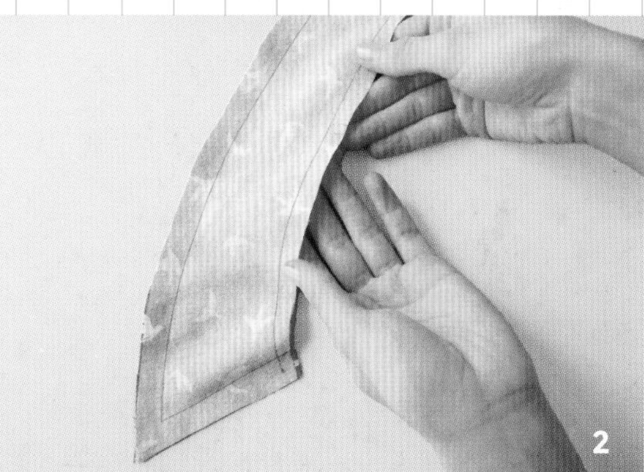

2 Place the top collar and undercollar pieces right sides together, and pin. Stitch along the short and outer edges, interfaced piece facing up, pivoting at the outer corners. Leave the inner edge unstitched (the line of stitching you can see on the inner edge is the staystitching you did earlier).

3 Trim the seam allowances. You can notch the outer edge allowances if you want to, but I prefer to trim them to about $\frac{3}{16}$" (4 mm) from the seamline. Snip or fold the corners and turn the collar right side out. From the right side, use a pin to gently pull the corners into points. Press the collar.

9 Understitch the seam allowances to the facing. Trim the seam allowances to about half their width. Using the tip of the iron, press the seam allowances open to help define a neat seamline. Now press the seam allowances away from the bodice and toward the facing. Understitch the seam allowances to the facing, close to the seamline to help prevent the facing from rolling to the outside of the blouse. Again, make sure the main part of the collar lies flat against the bodice and doesn't get caught in the stitching. You won't be able to understitch the corners at the top of the center front opening, so just stitch as far as you can on both the center front opening and the neckline.

10 Press the facing to the inside of the blouse. Fold the center front corners and turn the facing to the inside of the blouse. Press the collar to the outside and the facing to the inside of the blouse, rolling the seamline to the inside.

If you're worried about the facing rolling to the outside of the blouse, sew a few stitches in the ditch on the shoulder seams, either by hand or machine, to anchor the facing in place.

11 Sew the gathering stitches on the sleeve caps. Sew three rows of gathering stitches between the small circles on each sleeve cap.

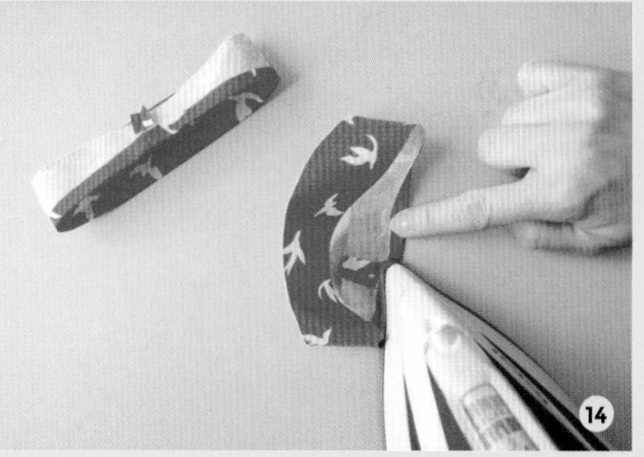

⓬ Make the pleats at the lower edge of the sleeves. On the right side of the sleeve, bring one of the full pleat lines to the parallel dashed line and press in place. Bring the other full pleat line to the other dashed line and press in place. Pin the pleats down. Repeat on the other sleeve, making sure the pleat formation on one sleeve is symmetrical to the other. Thread your machine in a contrasting color and set the stitch length to 3⁄16" (4 mm). Machine-baste across the pleats about 3⁄8" (1 cm) and 1½" (4 cm) from the edge.

⓭ Stitch the underarm seams. Rethread your machine in matching thread and reset the stitch length to 1⁄16–1⁄8" (1.5–3 mm). Join the underarm seams on each sleeve. If you want to use French seams, as I did, start by stitching the wrong sides together, using a ¼" (5 mm) seam allowance. Press the seam allowances open and then press the fabric around the seam allowance right sides together. Finally, stitch the seam with a 3⁄8" (1 cm) seam allowance.

Alternatively, you may want to sew the seam the standard way, right sides together, finishing the seam allowances using zigzag stitch or an overlocker. Now press the seam allowances toward the back.

⓮ Construct the sleeve facings. Apply iron-on interfacing to the sleeve facings with the iron. For each facing, place the short edges right sides together and stitch the seam to form a tube. Trim the seam allowances and press them open. Press under ¼" (5 mm) along the unnotched long edge, wrong sides together.

⓯ Pin and stitch the facings to the sleeves. Slip one sleeve facing over the lower end of one sleeve, right sides together and aligning the notched edges, and pin in place.

Turn the sleeve wrong side out. With the interfaced facing uppermost, stitch the facing to the sleeve, overlapping by a few stitches at the beginning and end. Repeat on the other sleeve.

16 Slipstitch the facing to the sleeve. Trim the seam allowances and press them open to help define a neat seamline. Remove the ⅜" (1 cm) row of machine-basting. Turn the facings to the inside of the sleeves, wrong sides together, and press, rolling the seamlines slightly to the inside. Slipstitch (page 173) the folded edge of the facings to the inside of the sleeves—or if you can't be bothered to hand sew them, topstitch by machine (sssshh! I won't tell!). Remove the 1½" (4 cm) row of machine-basting.

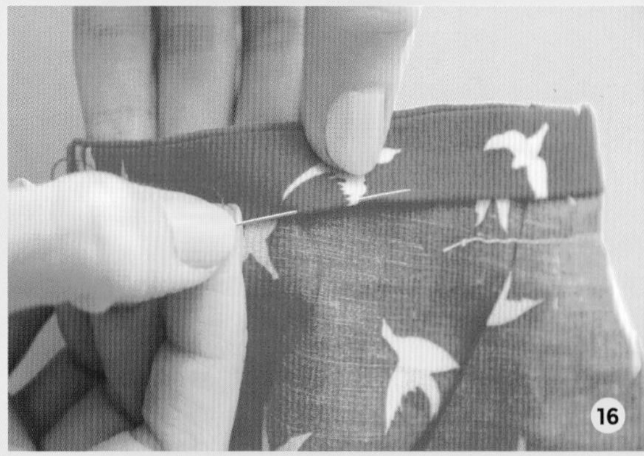
16

17 Stitch the sleeves to the bodice. Insert the sleeves into the bodice armholes, right sides together and matching notches, and pin. Pull up the gathers to fit and pin these, too. Thread your machine in a contrasting thread and set the stitch length to 3⁄16" (4 mm). Machine-baste each sleeve into its armhole. Once you're happy with your basting, rethread your machine in matching thread, reset your stitch length to 1⁄16–⅛" (1.5–3 mm), and sew the sleeves in place. Remove the gathering and basting stitches. Trim and finish the seam allowances using zigzag stitch or an overlocker. Press the seams, avoiding pressing the gathers.

17

18 Sew the hem of the blouse. The Mimi Blouse includes a 1¼" (3 cm) hem. Try the blouse on, pinning the center front closed at the fitting line (where the buttonholes will be), and adjust the hemline to ensure it's even all the way around. Fold the raw edge under by ⅝" (1.5 cm) and press. Fold under by another ⅝" (1.5 cm), press, and pin. Topstitch the hem in place, close to the upper fold.

18

19 Make the buttonholes. Stitch the buttonholes on the right front opening of the blouse (see the Buttonholes techniques, opposite and page 150).

19

BUTTONHOLES

TECHNIQUE

Learning to make buttonholes will open up a wonderful world of blouses, dresses, and more. There are various different types of buttonholes, and we're going to start with the machine-stitched variety.

A machine-stitched buttonhole is a thin rectangle with two long sides of tight zigzag stitches and bar tacks at either end. The center is then cut open to form the hole. Whether it's your first time or three millionth time sewing buttonholes, it's a good idea to make a test one first on a sample of your fabric (doubled over with interfacing in between) to check the thread tension and buttonhole length.

BUTTONHOLE PLACEMENT

Womenswear conventionally closes right over left, so the buttonholes will be stitched on the right opening. Mark your buttonholes in again if they've rubbed off since you cut out the fabric, clearly indicating the top and bottom of the hole (remember that the pattern includes ⅝"/1.5 cm seam allowances that you've now sewn). The buttonholes on the Mimi Blouse should line up with the point where the collar joins the neckline.

The Mimi Blouse has been designed for ½" (12 mm) buttons. If you want to use different-sized buttons, slightly larger or smaller is fine as long as they don't look out of proportion. Adjust the length of your buttonholes so they're ⅛" (3 mm) longer than the diameter of your button. If you want to play around with the position of the buttonholes—to sew them in pairs, for example—try to keep a buttonhole at the bust line to prevent any dodgy strain gaps in the front opening.

SEWING BUTTONHOLES

Different machines form buttonholes in different ways, usually either with a four-step buttonholer or an automatic buttonholer—now is a good time to get out your manual if you're not sure.

To sew a four-step buttonhole

I love four-step buttonholers—they may take a little more effort than their automatic counterparts, but you get more power over the way they turn out (control freak alert!). Set the stitch length as instructed in your manual. Attach the buttonhole foot and position it at the top end of the buttonhole. Move the slider on the foot so the window is just over the buttonhole marking and make sure the thread from your needle is laced through the window. Select buttonhole stitch 1 on your machine, and sew the left long side of the buttonhole until you reach the bottom of the marking, stopping with the needle on the left (you can use the handwheel to make individual stitches if you're finding it tricky to get your needle in the right place). Select buttonhole stitch 2/4 and slowly sew 5 stitches, stopping with the needle on the right. Select buttonhole stitch 3, and sew the right long side of the buttonhole (sewing backward) until you reach the top of the marking, stopping with the needle on the right. Select buttonhole stitch 2/4 again and sew a few stitches to complete the rectangle. Finally, select straight stitch and sew a couple of stitches over the end of the buttonhole to secure the threads.

To sew an automatic buttonhole

Wedge one of your buttons tightly into the holder at the back of the buttonholer foot to tell it how long to sew the buttonhole. Attach the foot to your machine and pull down the lever to the left of the needle as far as it will go. Select the buttonhole stitch function. Position the buttonhole foot over the marking on your fabric, with the needle at the bottom end of the marking. Start the machine and it'll sew the whole buttonhole for you—good times!

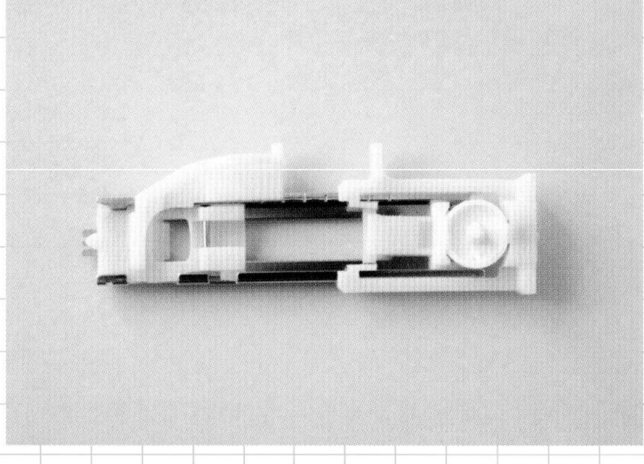

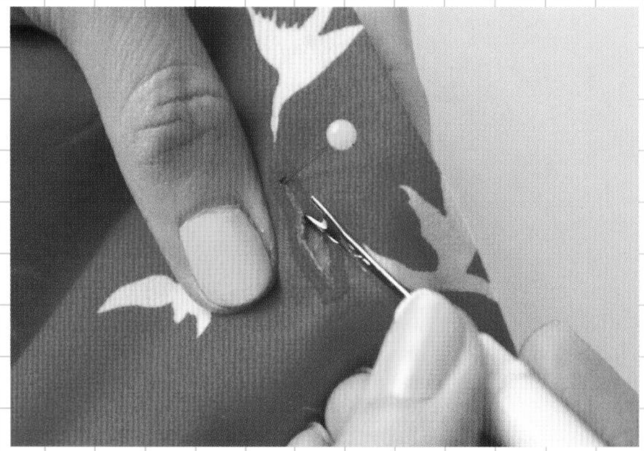

OPEN UP THE BUTTONHOLE

Using a seam ripper, carefully pierce the fabric between the buttonhole stitching at one end, then cut the fabric open toward the middle. Pierce the other end and cut toward the middle. Doing it in two stages will help avoid accidentally ripping through the stitching. If you have particularly wild tendencies with a seam ripper, you could put pins in either end of the buttonhole to act as stoppers.

⑳ **Sew the buttons to the blouse.** Mark the button positions on the left front opening and sew on the buttons (see the Sewing on Buttons technique, below).

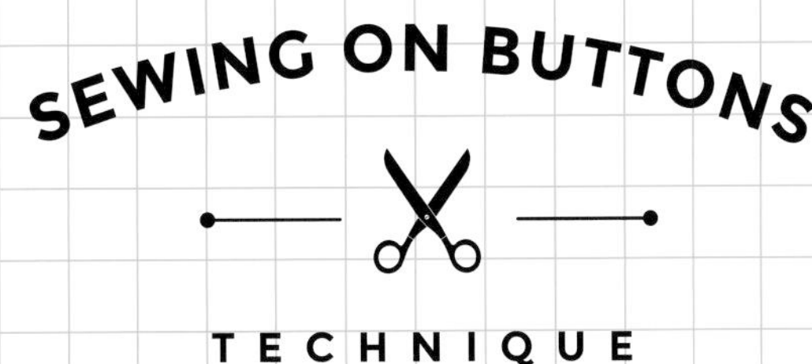

SEWING ON BUTTONS

TECHNIQUE

There's something so soothing about sitting down at the end of a sewing project to attach the buttons. I like to settle into the sofa with my favorite music playing and a cheeky drinkie—it's a dressmaker ritual.

1 Start by marking the position of the buttons on the left opening. Place the right side over the left as if you were doing up the blouse, lining up the neckline and hemline, and pin in place. Push the tip of a chalk pencil or washable pen through the buttonhole ⅛" (3 mm) down from the top end, and mark the position of each button with a little dot.

2 Thread a needle with about an arm's length of thread (any longer and it's more likely to get tangled up), double it, and tie the ends together in a knot. Make an initial stitch in your fabric at the button position, then attach the button to the outside of the garment, sewing through the holes in the button, or the shank, a few times. Finish on the inside of the garment, threading your needle through the stitches a couple of times to secure and finishing with a tight knot.

1

2

WAXED THREAD

If your thread keeps getting knotted up, applying thread wax can help it glide along more smoothly.

MAKE IT YOUR OWN

PIPING THE YOKE SEAMS

Piping can add a seriously pretty touch to seams, making your homemade clothes look that extra bit special.

You can make your own piping by cutting a long strip of fabric on the bias (diagonally across the fabric), wrapping it tightly around a strip of filler cord, and stitching it in place with a zipper foot. Personally, I prefer to buy ready-made piping to save time and fabric.

Here's how to insert piping into the front and back yoke seam on the Mimi Blouse.

1. Cut strips of piping just a little longer than the length of the top and bottom seams of the yoke. Trim down the yoke seam allowances to the width of the flat part of the piping. Place the piping against the right side of the fabric, aligning raw edges, with the piping on the stitching line, and pin in place.
2. Using a zipper foot (or a dedicated piping foot if you have one), machine-baste the piping seam to the yoke seam, as close as you can get to the piping cord.
3. Gather the seams on the front and back bodice as normal, and pin to the yoke, right sides together, with the piping sandwiched in between. Still using a zipper or piping foot, stitch the seams—or machine-baste first if you want to—getting as close as you can to the piping cord. This is the key here—get seriously up close and personal with that piping cord, without stitching through it. You can push the piping cord right up against the presser foot with your fingers if you need to. Get in there!
4. Trim off the ends of the piping to fit the seams, remove the gathering stitches, and admire your beautiful piped seams!

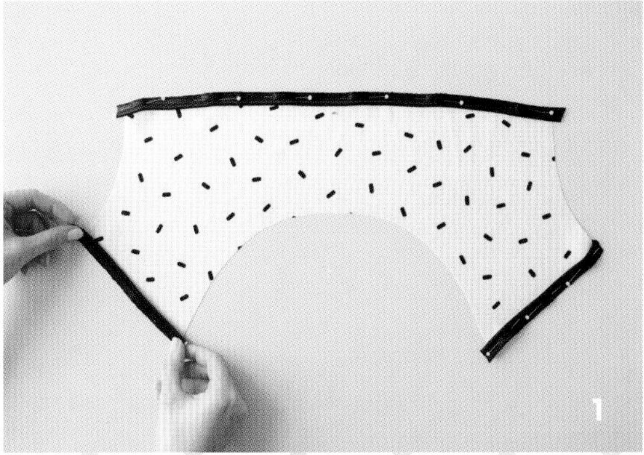
1

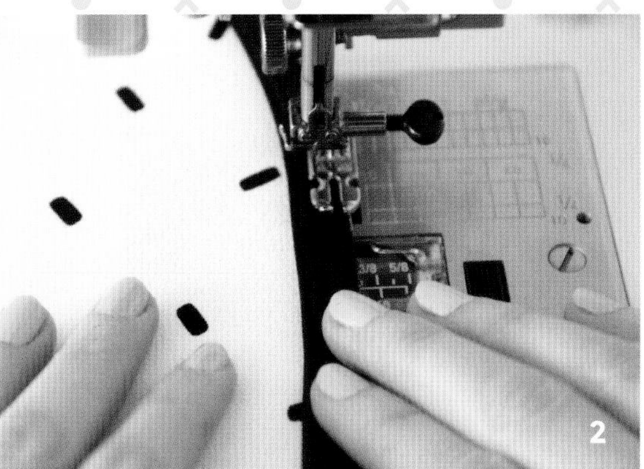
2

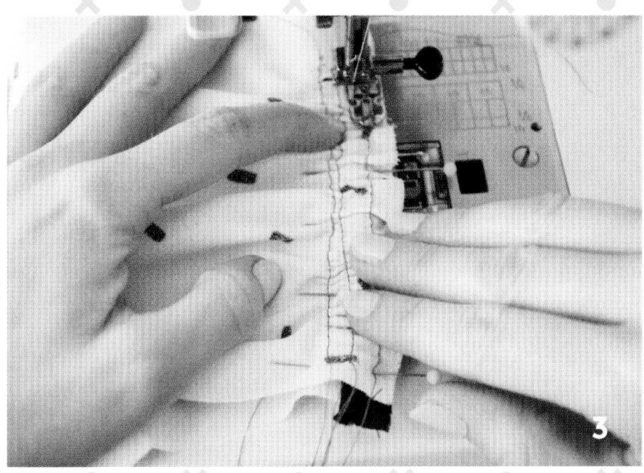
3

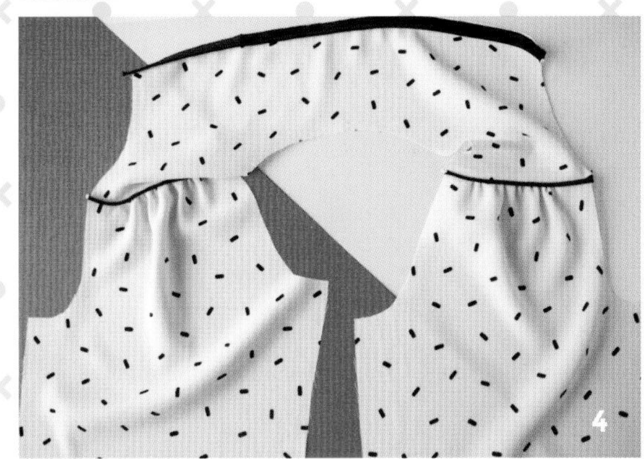
4

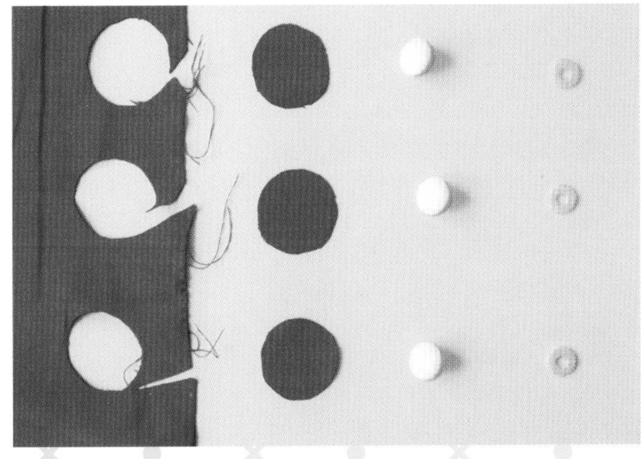

FABRIC-COVERED BUTTONS

I simply adore fabric-covered buttons. The subtlety of a button made in the same fabric as the garment is oh-so stylish. You can also make them in contrasting colors or patterns, opening up a world of possibility that often surpasses the range of regular buttons on offer in a store. Play around with different color combinations to create something unique.

To make fabric-covered buttons you will need self-cover button molds, which you can buy from most craft stores or notions departments. They come in various different sizes and in plastic or metal.

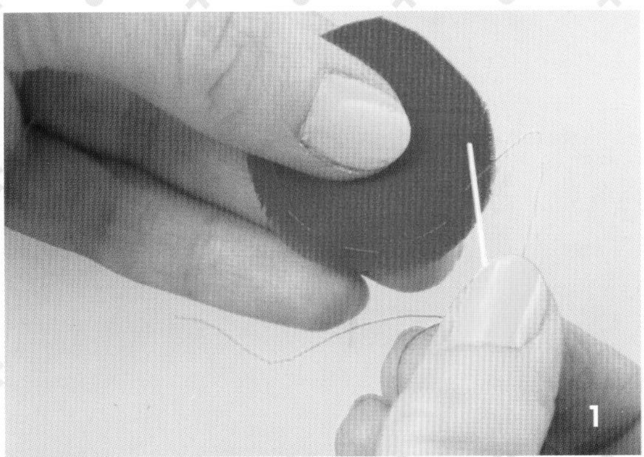

1

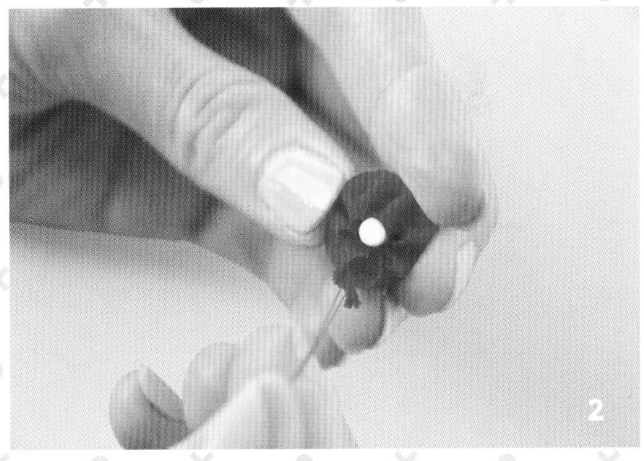

2

1. For each button, cut a circle of fabric just less than double the diameter of the button itself. (The back of the button packet may include a template to use when cutting the circles.) The button molds have front and back pieces—wedge them apart if they came joined together.

   Thread a needle without knotting it, and sew long stitches by hand around the circumference of the fabric, leaving a length of thread at each end.

2. Center the front piece of the self-cover button against the wrong side of the fabric, and gently pull on both ends of the thread to gather the fabric around it. Pull reeeeally tightly, smoothing out any ridges in the fabric.

3 Push on the button back to secure the fabric in place. You may need a tool such as pliers to push the button back down tightly. I find a thread spool works perfectly—place the end over the back of the button and press down.

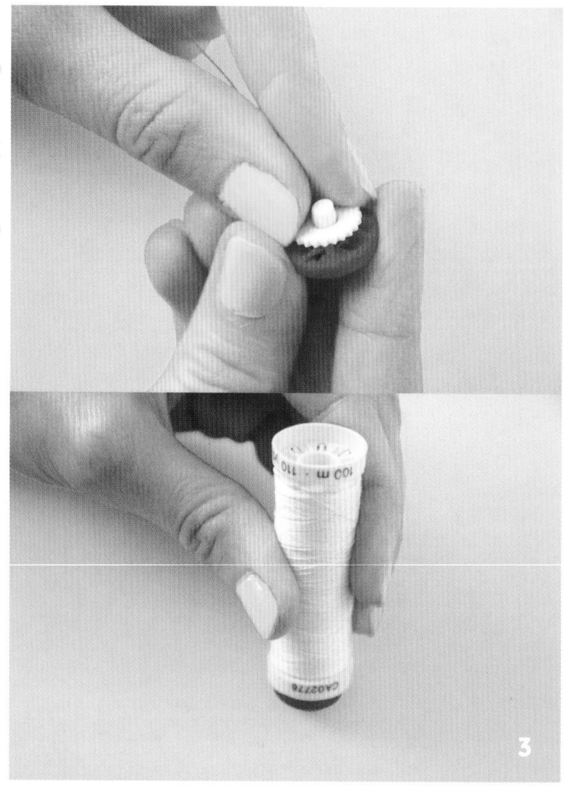

And there's your finished button!

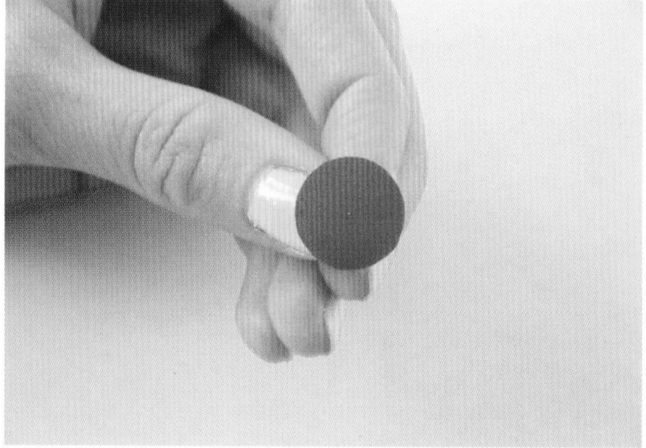

SOME MORE IDEAS...

- Make the collar in a contrasting color.
- Position the buttons and buttonholes in pairs.
- Sew sequins, studs, or motifs onto the end of the collar.
- Redraw the collar into a Peter Pan shape.
- Tie a ribbon around the neckline.

MAKE IT A LIFESTYLE

DRESSING HANDMADE

You've poured hours of time and buckets of love into your sewing project. So now you want to wear it! As much as possible! And show the world that you're a DIY dressmaker and proud!

Yet it's so easy to fall into the trap of making something that you wear once and swiftly banish to the back of the closet. I used to do this all the time when I started sewing. The problem was that I got so overexcited at all the possibilities of things that I could make, that I didn't really stop to consider whether what I was making was really "me." I took so much pleasure in making a Betty Draper-style dress, for example, but once I'd finished it I realized it swamped my frame, didn't fit with the rest of my wardrobe, and really wasn't very practical for running for the bus. While it was fun to make, I really wasn't going to get much wear out of it.

So how can you ensure that you'll be happy wearing your handmade clothing on a daily basis? As well as choosing fabrics appropriate to the garment (page 44) and taking the time to make it fit you, there are some other important points to consider.

SEW FOR YOUR LIFESTYLE

Making fancy frocks is lots of fun, and it's a wonderful feeling to turn up at a party wearing something that you made yourself and that you know for a fact no one else will be wearing. But if you want handmade to be part of your regular lifestyle, make some stuff that you're actually going to wear on a daily basis. Do you spend most of your time sitting at a desk, playing with small children, standing behind a shop counter, presenting to clients at power meetings? What kinds of outfits make you feel comfortable in your everyday routine? A great way of working this out is thinking about which clothes in your closet you miss when they're in the laundry basket. Make more things like that and you'll soon be wearing handmade every day.

MAKE CLOTHES THAT SUIT YOU

I love keeping up with which sewing patterns are hot right now and seeing all the lovely creations that people make with them. But I'm also very aware that a dress that looks amazing on my six-foot-tall Brazilian babe friend, Rachel, is probably going to look ridiculous on moi. And that's fine. Be honest with yourself about which silhouettes complement your body shape and which are best left to your fellow DIY dressmakers. Consider colors, too—when choosing fabrics, pick tones that make your face look radiant rather than washed out. If you really can't resist a fabric but know it won't suit you, you can always show your love in other ways—by making it into a pillow cover, for example.

BE CONFIDENT IN YOUR SIGNATURE STYLE

Now that you can make your own clothes, you no longer need to rely on the stores with their ever-changing collections as trends come and go. Instead, you can develop a longer-term signature style that makes you feel comfortable, confident, and authentic—a style that feels right for you. Have a think about who your style icons are and what it is about the way they dress that you admire. Which colors make you happiest? Do you favor graphic, floral, or animal prints? Set up a physical or online scrapbook to document the looks that you love, and whittle it down until you see a theme emerging—that should give you a big clue as to how to define your signature style. If you're not already dressing that way regularly, now you can set about turning it into a reality by sewing clothing that makes you excited to get dressed every morning.

KEEP IT COMPLEMENTARY

Related to the point above about developing a signature style, a smart sewing strategy would be to stick to a particular color palette. If your handmade tops go with your self-stitched skirts, you'll find it so much easier to pick out your daily outfits. This doesn't necessarily mean you have to limit yourself to sewing with the neutrals so often associated with the idea of the "capsule wardrobe." I mean, if beige is your thing, then go with it, but a palette of jewel tones, pastels, or primary colors (the latter being my personal palette of choice, as you may have noticed) works equally well.

PRACTICE WEARING HANDMADE

A great way of training yourself to make more clothes that you love is to get into the habit of wearing the clothes that you've made as much as you can. Try giving yourself a challenge to dress handmade regularly. This might be once a week when you're just starting to build up your handmade wardrobe, or join in with one of the online events such as Me Made May, which sees hundreds of DIY dressmakers donning their homemade frocks for a whole month. Not only will you enjoy the experience of wearing your craft with pride, but the more you do it, the more you'll realize which kinds of makes you like wearing the most. Make more of these things, and less of the things that you don't naturally reach for when you get dressed.

Keep these strategies up and you'll always have something to wear.

LILOU DRESS

CHAPTER 7

Take your dressmaking skills to the next level with the gorgeous Lilou Dress. It features a chic scoop neckline at both front and back, a stunning pleated skirt, and a lined, darted bodice that creates an elegant finish on the inside as well as outside. Dress it up with your bow belt for a party, layer it over a blouse for the office, or wear it with a stripy top on weekends.

SUPPLIES

2¼ yd (2 m) length of fashion fabric, 60" (150 cm) wide

⅝ yd (50 cm) length of lining fabric, 60" (150 cm) wide

OR 1 yd (1 m) length of lining fabric, 45" (115 cm) wide

16" (40 cm) invisible zipper (in color to match your fabric)

Thread (in color to match your fabric and lining)

TOOLS

See page 14

Zipper foot

Invisible zipper foot

OPTIONAL

Iron-on interfacing in similar weight to your fabric (page 175)

TECHNIQUES

Setting up your sewing machine (page 21)

Stitching school (page 26)

Pinning (page 30)

Adjusting stitches (page 32)

Choosing your fabric (page 44)

Preparing your pattern (page 47)

Laying out fabric and pattern (page 48)

Cutting out fabric pieces (page 50)

Understanding clothing construction (page 54)

Simple seam allowance finishes (page 55)

Pressing matters (page 57)

Hemming (page 60)

Pattern sizing (page 72)

Interfacing (page 77)

Inserting an invisible zipper (page 80)

Fitting your garment (page 96)

Staystitching (page 99)

Shaping with darts and dart tucks (page 100)

Attaching a neckline facing (page 104)

Stitch in the ditch (page 128)

Lining a garment (page 168)

Fashioning pleats (page 170)

Slipstitching (page 173)

FABRIC SUGGESTIONS

Choose a fabric with body to give the pleats some structure—try medium-weight cotton (including poplin, sateen, chambray, and gabardine) or linen. A solid color will show off the pleats best. A drapey polyester, lightweight cotton, or crepe will create a more relaxed silhouette, working particularly well for the gathered skirt variation (page 176). Note that the pleated skirt needs fabric 60" (150 cm) wide.

For the lining, a lightweight to medium-weight cotton (including poplin, lawn, and batiste) will be easier to sew than dedicated lining fabric. If you're sewing the shell in a drapey fabric, you could use the same on the inside. Alternatively, choose a contrasting lining for a surprise when you—or that special someone—unzip the dress.

PATTERN DETAILS

The paper pattern has 4 pieces:
Front bodice—cut 1 fashion fabric on the fold + 1 lining on the fold
Back bodice—cut 2 fashion fabric + 2 lining
Front skirt—cut 1 fashion fabric on the fold
Back skirt—cut 2 fashion fabric

Seam allowance is ⅝" (1.5 cm).

PATTERN SIZING

BODY MEASUREMENTS

SIZE	BUST	WAIST	HIP
1	30" (76 cm)	24" (61 cm)	33" (84 cm)
2	32" (81 cm)	26" (66 cm)	35" (89 cm)
3	34" (86.5 cm)	28" (71 cm)	37" (94 cm)
4	36" (91.5 cm)	30" (76 cm)	39" (99 cm)
5	38" (96.5 cm)	32" (81 cm)	41" (104 cm)
6	40" (101.5 cm)	34" (86.5 cm)	43" (109 cm)
7	42" (106.5 cm)	36" (91.5 cm)	45" (114 cm)
8	44" (112 cm)	38" (96.5 cm)	47" (119.5 cm)

FINISHED GARMENT MEASUREMENTS

SIZE	BUST	WAIST
1	32" (81 cm)	25" (63.5 cm)
2	34" (86.5 cm)	27" (68.5 cm)
3	36" (91.5 cm)	29" (73.5 cm)
4	38" (96.5 cm)	31" (79 cm)
5	40" (101.5 cm)	33" (84 cm)
6	42" (106.5 cm)	35" (89 cm)
7	44" (112 cm)	37" (94 cm)
8	46" (117 cm)	39" (99 cm)

Back length (nape to waistline) = 16¾" (42.5 cm)

FABRIC LAYOUT

Here is the suggested arrangement of the pattern pieces on the fabric.

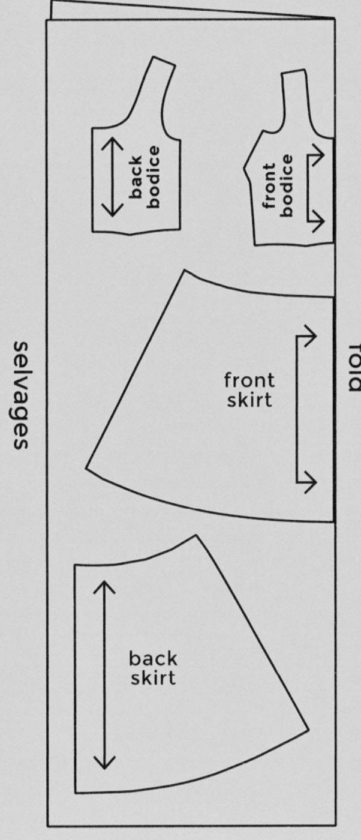

60" (150 cm) wide fabric only

TO MAKE THE DRESS

1 Make a toile of the bodice. Adjust the toile to fit your shape, then make any changes to your paper pattern. Cut your fashion fabric and lining pieces and transfer the markings, including adding the pleat marking lines on the right side of the skirt pieces. Snip notches in the seam allowances in the center of the neckline of the front bodice and front lining.

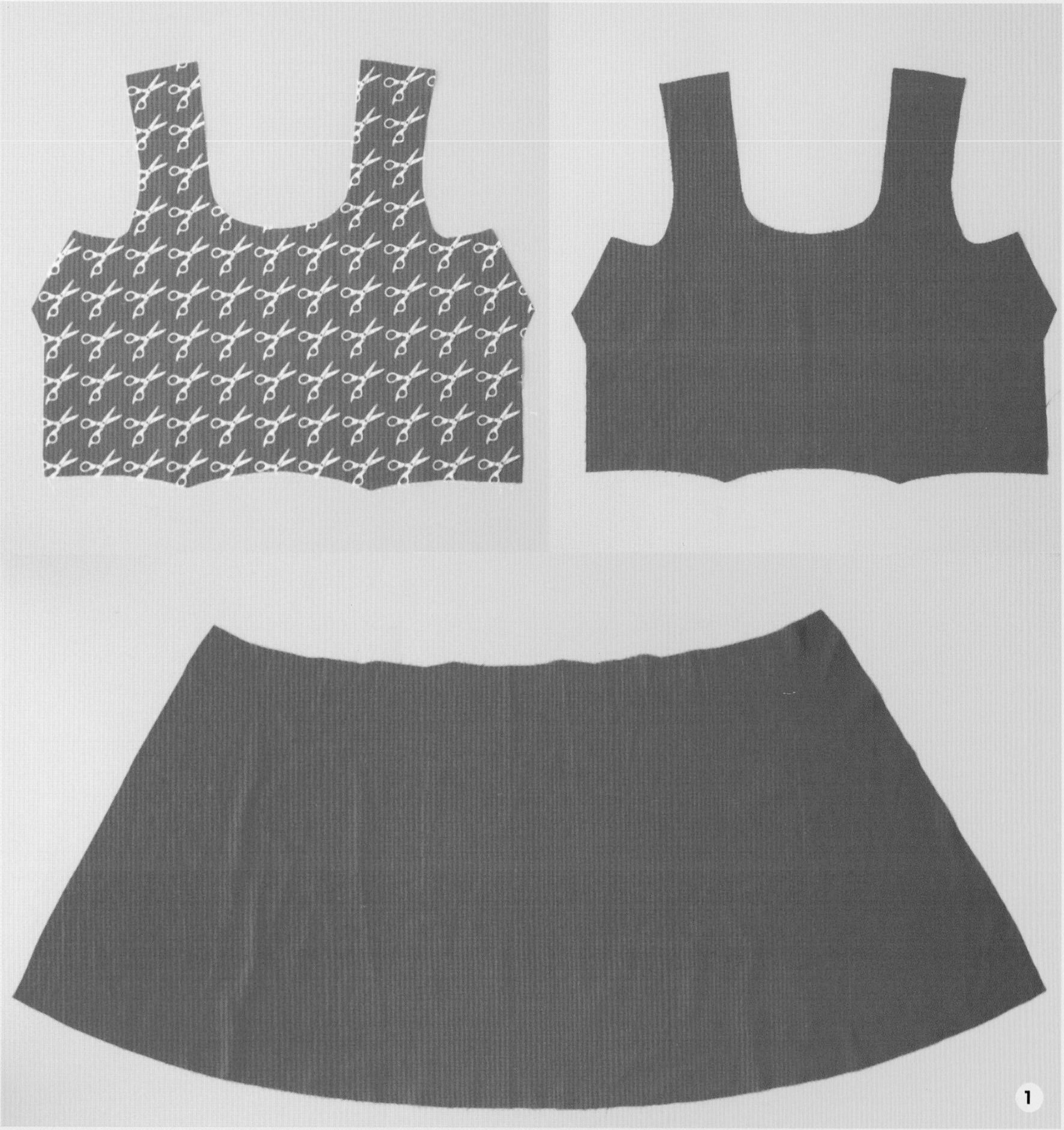

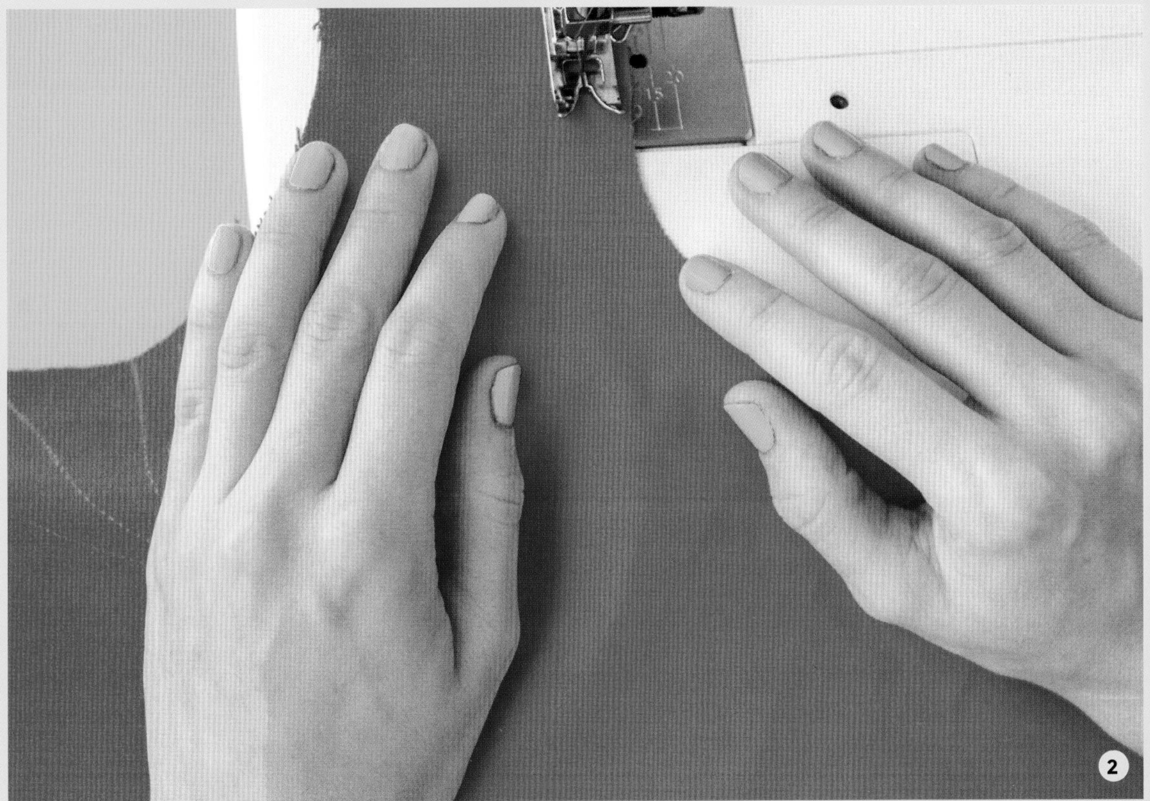

2 Staystitch the neckline on the front and back fashion fabric bodice pieces. Stitch from each shoulder to the center, ⅜" (1 cm) from the raw edge.

3 Stitch the darts on the front and back bodice. Press the bust darts downward and the waistline darts toward the center on both the wrong and right sides of the fabric.

4 Pin the shoulder seams, right sides together. Stitch the seams, trim, and press the seam allowances open. There's no need to finish the bodice seams; the lining will hide them—hooray!

LINING A GARMENT

TECHNIQUE

Lining a garment takes a little extra effort, but the benefits make it worthwhile for some items.

- It hides the raw edges inside the garment, providing an elegant alternative to finishing seams—particularly great when you have messy seams such as on Lilou's pleated skirt.
- It adds a comfortable layer that feels lovely against your skin and glides on and off easily.
- It adds weight or warmth to lighter fabrics.
- Lining fabric reduces transparency.
- It makes the dressmaker feel really smug that the inside of the garment looks as pretty as the outside!

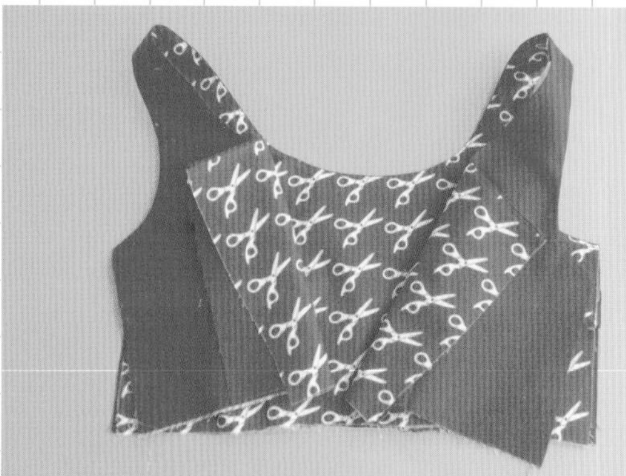

❺ **Construct the bodice lining.** Trim the neckline of the front and back lining by ⅛" (3 mm), to entice the lining to roll to the inside when pressed. Construct the lining in the same way as the bodice, including pressing darts and shoulder seams.

❻ **Join the bodice and lining at the neck.** Pin the lining to the bodice around the neckline, right sides together and matching shoulder seams and center front notches. Stitch right around the neckline.

5

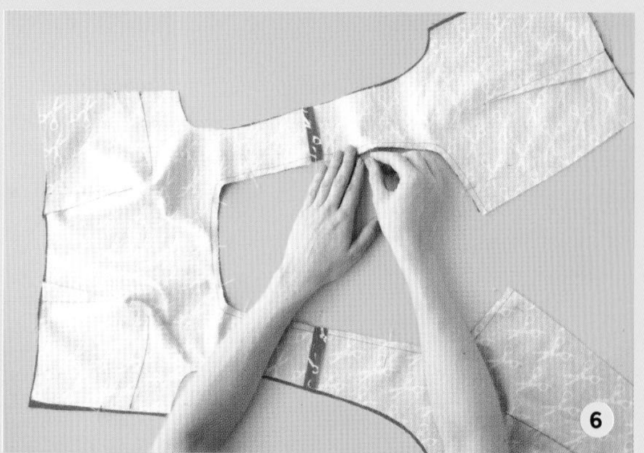

6

❼ **Understitch the seam allowances to the lining.** Press the seam allowances and lining away from the bodice. With the seam allowances uppermost, understitch the seam allowances to the lining, close to the seamline, all around the neckline. Trim the seam allowances close to the understitching.

❽ **Join the bodice and lining at the armholes.** Pin the lining to the bodice at the armholes, right sides together and matching the lining shoulder seams to bodice shoulder seams. Stitch around both armholes. Understitch the armhole seam allowances to the lining, close to the seamline—you won't be able to get right into the shoulders, but stitch as far as you can. Trim the seam allowances close to the understitching.

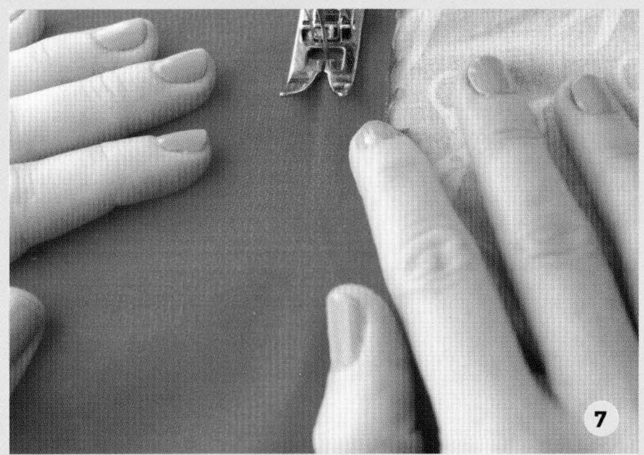
7

❾ **Turn the bodice right side out.** Now for some magic: gently pull each back bodice piece right through its shoulder to turn the whole bodice right side out. This may take a bit of patience—and possibly a chopstick or similarly shaped implement—but it'll soon be the right side out. Press the bodice, rolling the lining slightly to the inside so the seamline is not visible from the right side.

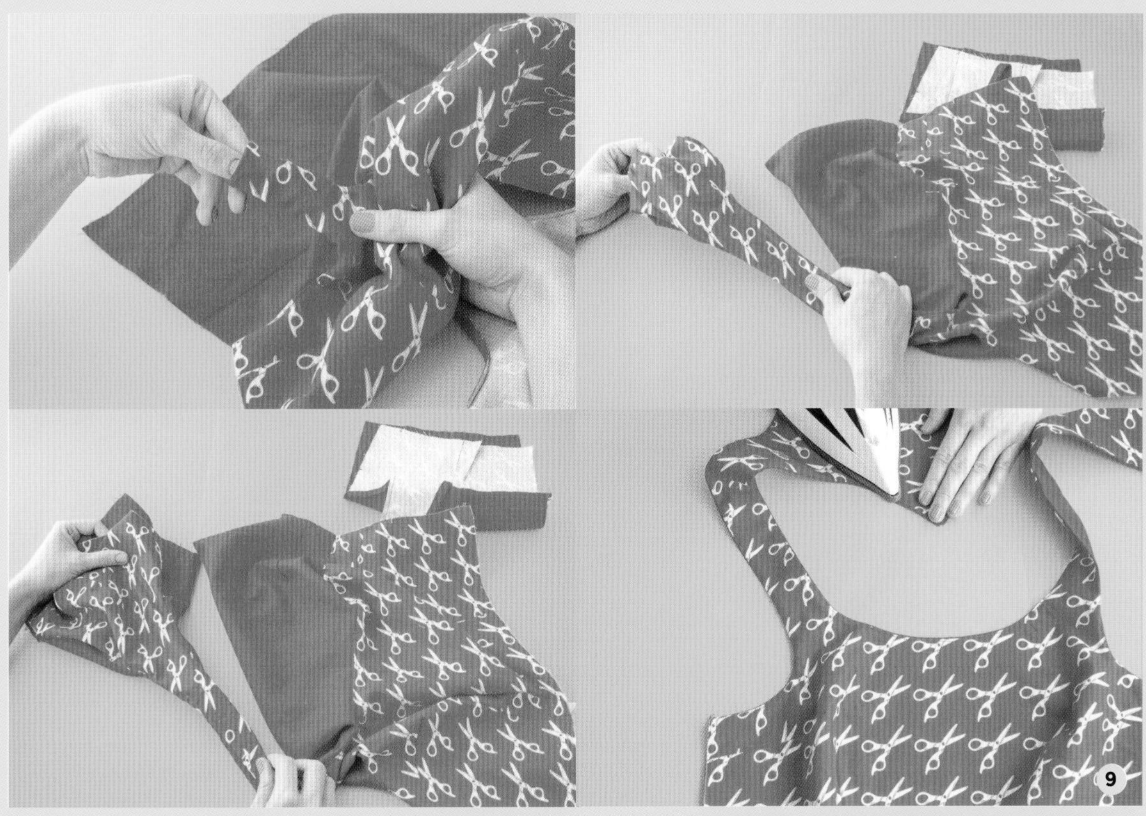
9

⑩ Finish the bodice. Place the front and back bodice pieces right sides together at the side seams. Pull the front and back linings up and away from the bodice. Pin the front and back bodice at the side seams, then pin the front and back lining at the side seams, matching the seams where the bodice meets the lining. Stitch in one continuous line down one bodice and lining side seam. Repeat on the other side seam. Trim the seam allowances and press them open.

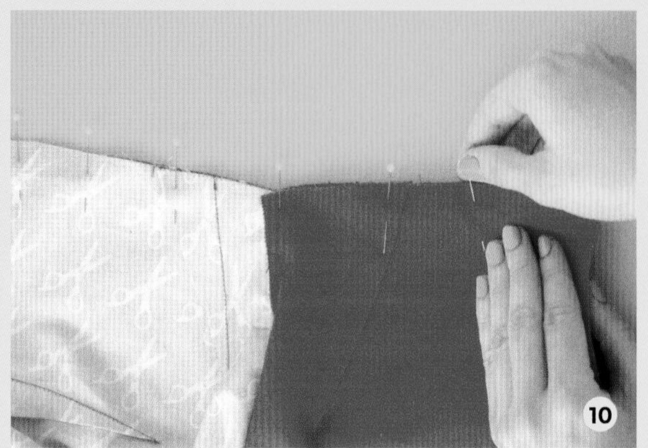

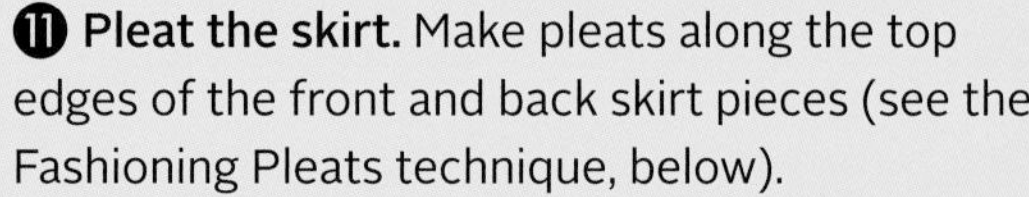

⑪ Pleat the skirt. Make pleats along the top edges of the front and back skirt pieces (see the Fashioning Pleats technique, below).

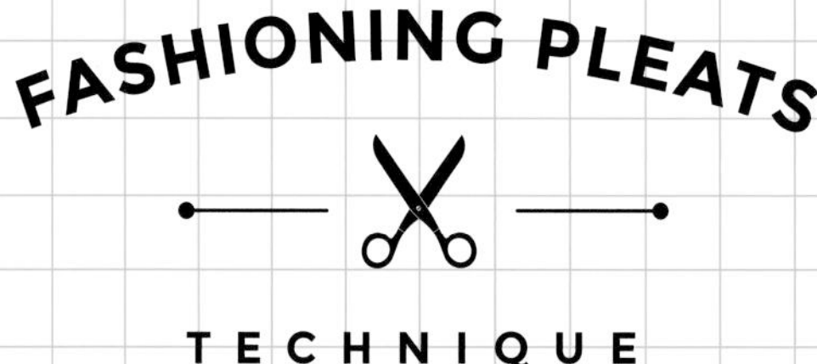

FASHIONING PLEATS

TECHNIQUE

Pleats are a great alternative to gathering for adding fullness to a skirt. Fashioning neat pleats takes a little care but isn't too tricky to achieve.

1 From the right side, fold the fabric wrong sides together along each longer pleat marking and pin. Using a contrasting thread and setting your stitch length to ³⁄₁₆" (4 mm), machine-baste about 2" (5 cm) down the pleat, close to the fold, to hold it in place. Press each fold.

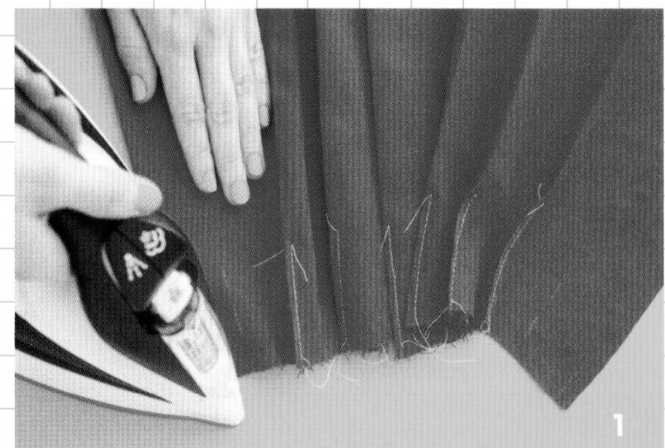

CHECKING FIT

When folding a lot of fabric into pleats, the length of the skirt waistline can increase or decrease a bit. Before going further, align the skirt with the bodice, matching the bodice waistline darts to the center front skirt pleats. Check the side seams and adjust if necessary.

2 Bring the basted pleats to meet the shorter pleat marking, following the direction of the arrows. Pin the pleats in place. Machine-baste horizontally across the pleats, all the way along the top edge of the skirt pieces, ⅜" (1 cm) from the edge. Press the tops of the pleats.

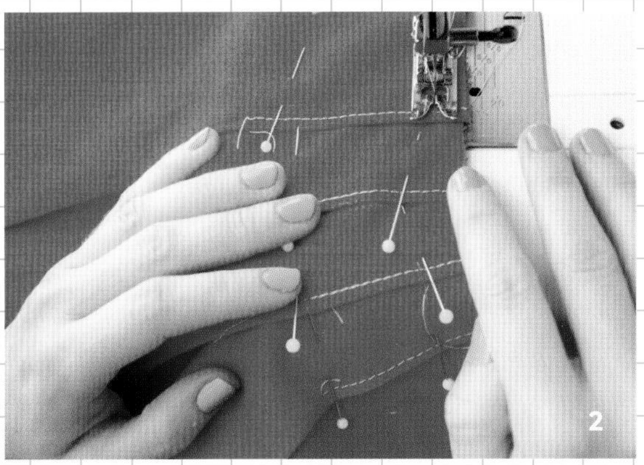

⓬ **Stitch the skirt side seams.** Pin the skirt front to the skirt back pieces at the side seams, right sides together and matching notches. Stitch the seams, then trim, finish and press the seam allowances either open or toward the back.

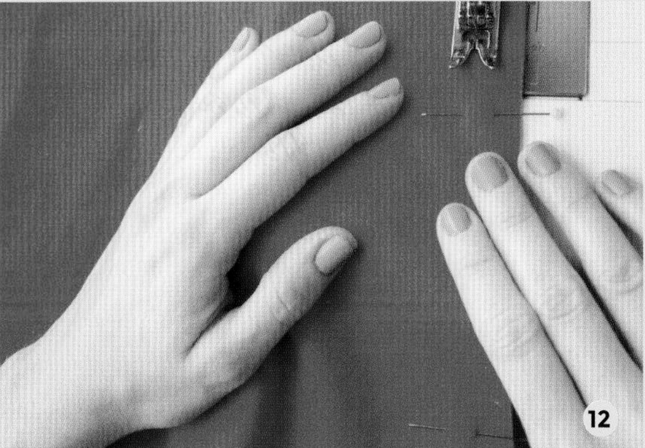

⓭ **Join the bodice to the skirt.** Pull the bodice lining up and out of the way. Pin the bodice to the skirt at the waistline, right sides together, matching side seams, and aligning the waistline darts with the pleat lines at each side of center front. Stitch the seams, then trim the seam allowances and press them toward the bodice. Remove the machine-basting.

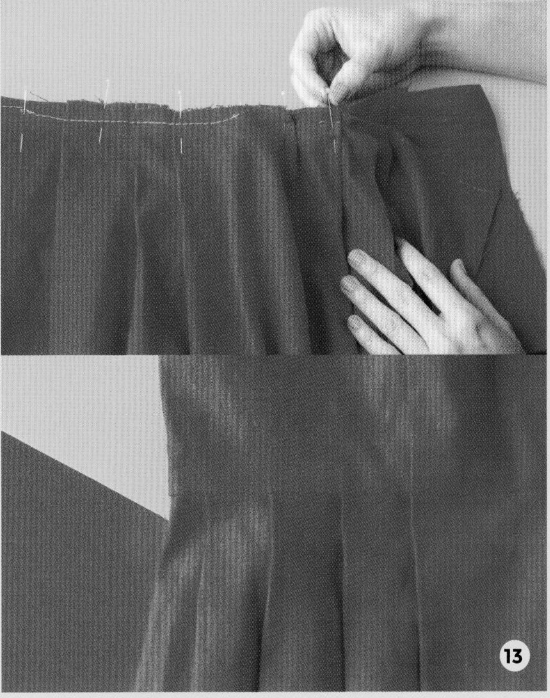

HEAVY FABRIC

If you're using a heavy fabric that will be pulling on this waistline seam with its weight, you could reinforce it with an extra row of stitching.

⓮ Insert the zipper into the center back opening. Check the fit of the dress and adjust the center back seams if necessary. With the lining pulled out of the way, press the back opening seams to mark where the zipper teeth should go (on the bodice and skirt only, not the lining). Finish the back opening seams. Align the top stop of the invisible zipper with the neckline at center back and pin in place. Keeping the lining out of the way, insert the invisible zipper using an invisible zipper foot. Stitch the rest of the seam using a regular zipper foot. Press the seam allowances open.

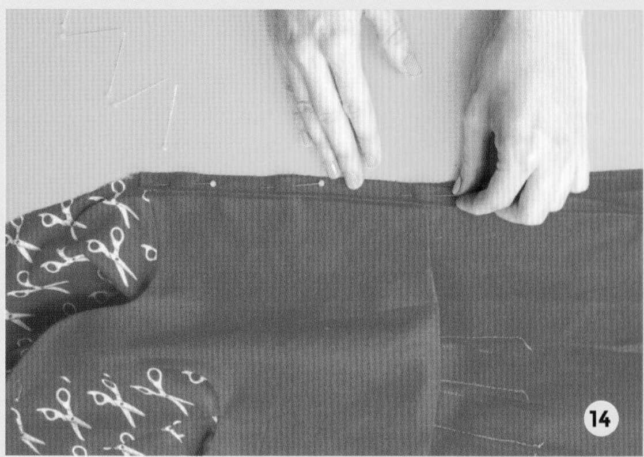

⓯ Finish attaching the lining. Press under ⅝" (1.5 cm) along the bottom edge of the lining—so it just reaches the waistline seam when attached to the bodice. Open the zipper. Turn the lining to the outside of the bodice, right sides together, and pin the raw edges of the back seams to the bodice back seams and zipper tapes. Using a zipper foot, and keeping the bottom of the lining turned up, stitch close to the zipper teeth.

⓰ Slipstitch the lining to bodice at the waistline. Turn the lining back to the inside of the dress, folding the corners neatly. Slipstitch the bottom of the lining to the bodice waistline seam (see the Slipstitching technique, opposite). Press the edge.

SLIPSTITCHING

TECHNIQUE

Slipstitching is an almost invisible hand stitch, used to join a folded edge (such as the turned-under edge of the Lilou bodice lining) to another piece of fabric (such as the seam allowances of the Lilou bodice). Sewing by hand obviously takes a lot longer than by machine, but I find the slow, repetitive action can be calming and therapeutic. Put your favorite music on, pour yourself a drink, settle down, and prepare to become Zen.

To work slipstitch, first thread a needle with a long piece of thread knotted at one end. Insert the needle through the folded edge and make a short stitch along the fold. Take a tiny stitch in the fabric the folded edge is being sewn to, close to the fold where the needle came out, and pull the layers together. Take another longer stitch (about ¼"/5 mm) through the fold, then a tiny stitch in the other fabric layer. Continue in this way to join the edges together.

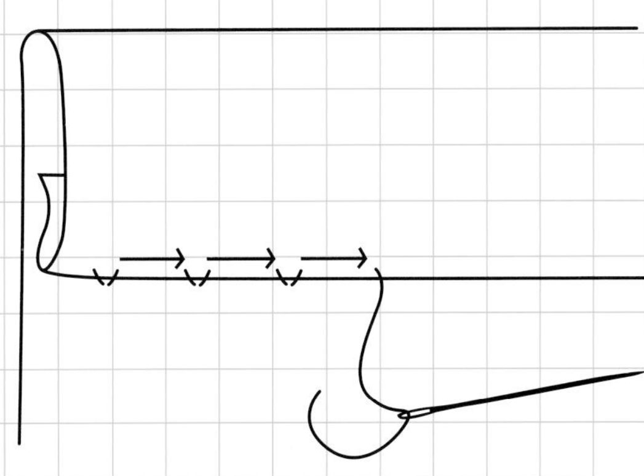

LET IT HANG

If you can resist the urge to finish the dress right now, it's sensible to let it hang overnight before hemming it in case it stretches—particularly if your fabric is fairly heavy.

⑰ Hem the dress. The Lilou Dress includes a 1¼" (3 cm) hem. Try the dress on and adjust the hemline to your preference using pins. Turn under the hem by ⅝" (1.5 cm) and press. Turn under another ⅝" (1.5 cm), press, and pin. Topstitch the hem in place.

Give the dress a final press, and then break out the cocktails!

MAKE IT YOUR OWN

SCULPT A SCALLOP NECKLINE

All this variation really requires is a bit of stitching precision and some hardcore pressing action. Practice sewing scallops on some scrap fabric first and you'll soon get the hang of it. Once you've grasped the principle of adding scallop shaping to a pattern, it's easy to add the detail to other sewing projects, too.

YOU WILL NEED

- Lilou Dress pattern and supplies
- Paper and pencil
- Round-bottomed object, such as a food can or glass
- Dressmaker's carbon and tracing wheel
- Iron-on interfacing

1 Trace the front bodice of the Lilou Dress onto a new piece of paper. Using your round-bottomed object as a template, draw two scallops along the neckline, avoiding the top of the shoulder straps. Remember that your pattern includes seam allowance, so the finished scallops will be smaller. This is your new pattern piece for both bodice and lining. Cut out your fabric, then trim the lining by ⅛" (3 mm) to help it roll to the inside of the dress.

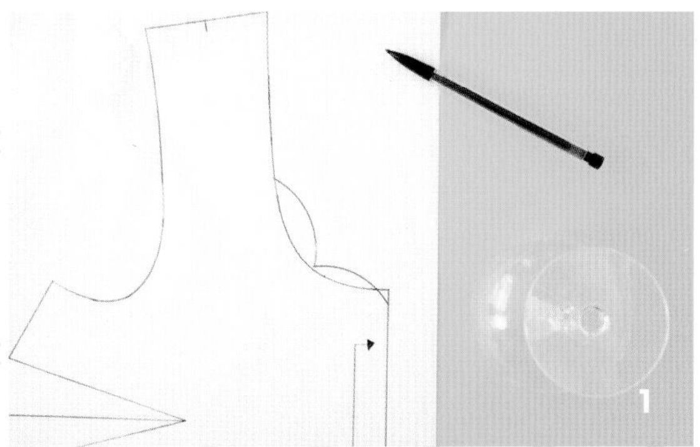

1

2 Cut a narrow piece of iron-on interfacing to the shape of the front neckline—this will help reinforce the scallops. Attach the interfacing to the neckline of the front lining with the iron.

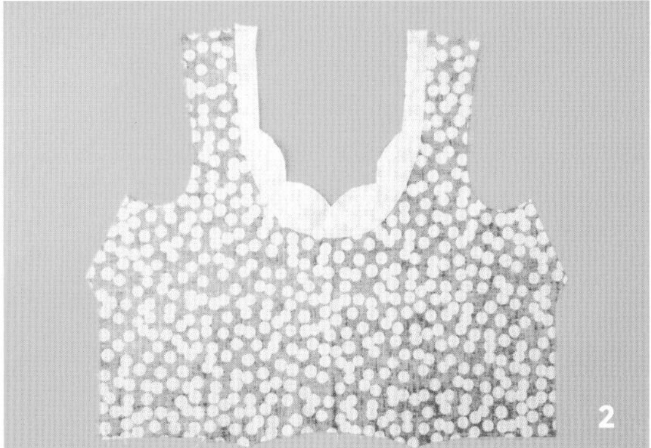

2

3 Construct the bodice following the regular instructions up to the neckline stitching stage, Step 6. To attach the front bodice to the lining at the neckline, set your stitch length to about ¹⁄₁₆" (1.5 mm)—the smaller stitches will help navigate those curves. Stitch along the scallop line slowwwly and smooooothly, pivoting the needle at the inner corner of each scallop. Reinforce the inner corners with a few extra stitches.

3

4 Trim the seam allowances down to about ¼" (5 mm). Cut triangular-shaped notches into the seam allowances around the outer edges of the curves and at the points where the scallops meet, cutting close to the stitching line but not through it. (If you do accidentally cut through the thread, it's not the end of the world—just go over that bit again with some new stitching.)

5 Now comes the hardcore pressing action—this will help get those curves nice and smooth. With right sides still together, run the point of your iron right up and along the seamline between the layers. Turn the bodice right side out, and repeat on the inside. Again, you want to roll the lining slightly to the inside—use the steam on your iron to make the fabric more malleable.

Done! Seriously sexy scallops to make you smile. You can now stitch the rest of the dress as normal.

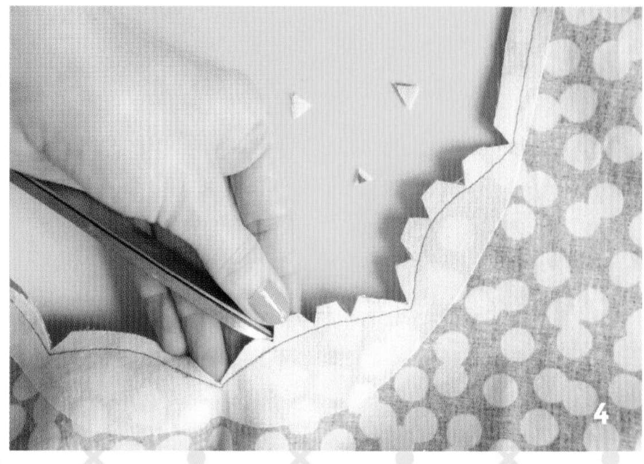

4

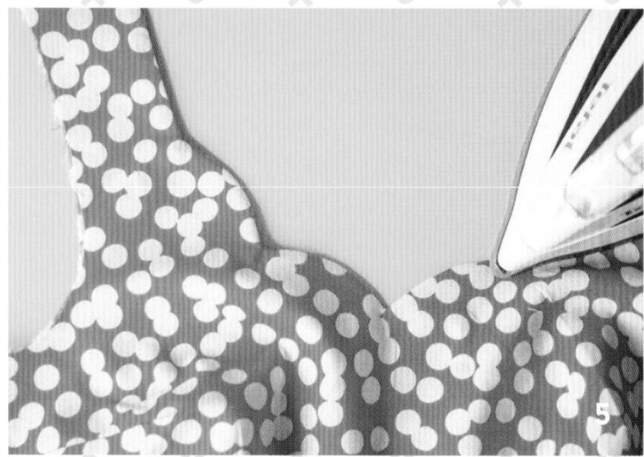

5

SOME MORE IDEAS...

- Make a bow belt in a matching fabric (page 133).
- Stitch buttons down the front of the bodice (page 88).
- Attach decorative ribbon to the bodice or hem (page 112).
- Make the bodice and skirt in contrasting fabrics.

GATHERED SKIRT

It's easy to change the skirt to a gathered version for a softer look. Simply use the front and back skirt pieces from your self-drafted Clémence Skirt pattern (page 116), attaching them to the Lilou bodice instead of the waistband.

MAKE IT A LIFESTYLE

SEWING SOLO, SEWING SOCIALLY

SEWING SOLO

One of the best things about sewing ("Yet another thing?!" you cry) is that you don't need to go anywhere special to do it. I worked with arts venues for many years, and we were constantly grappling with the issue of how to entice people to travel to us, to book a ticket for an event, and to interact with the art. There's no such issue with sewing—you can participate with the craft in your own home, whenever you get the urge and are inherently engaged with the process. You don't even need to get dressed.

Making time to be alone with your sewing machine is a wonderful way to relax and get some head space from day-to-day tasks and concerns. Settle down with some music and a cup of tea, zone out from your usual thought processes, focus on the task of making, and get into the creative flow. Before you know it, it'll be after nightfall, you're still wearing your pajamas from the night before, and you feel amazing.

SEWING SOCIALLY

Sewing doesn't always have to be a solo activity though. Meeting other dressmaking buffs is a great way of sharing tips, finding out about the latest patterns, and keeping you inspired and motivated to create. Try setting up a Craft Club with friends for an afternoon of making and conviviality—if you don't want to schlep your machine around, you could bring hand sewing or hold a Sew 'n' Tell with your finished projects. Or visit a sewing café—more and more venues are springing up where you can hire a sewing machine by the hour, eat some cake, and share a giggle.

The Internet has opened up a whole new way of sewing socially, creating an online sewing circle of people of all ages and backgrounds from all over the world. Sewing bloggers are a friendly bunch, so join in the conversation by commenting on blog posts, joining a #SewingSocial Twitter chat, or consider starting your own blog. Keep an eye out for the next meet-up, where everyone is welcome to come along to a group fabric-shopping session or field trip to a special event. Meet-ups often involve a fabric swap, so bring along any fabric you no longer want and prepare to go home laden with goodies, as well as wonderful new friendships.

WHAT NEXT?

Now that you've "graduated" from this book, what can you do next? The patterns are versatile enough to be made again and again in different fabrics and with different variations. By now you'll also have the skills, understanding, and confidence to start making a whole world of other dressmaking projects. You may also be itching to learn new techniques to take your sewing to the next level.

8401
Size 14
50c
Simplicity PRINTED Pattern
proportioned for teens
SUB-TEEN
8S 10S 12S 14S
TEEN
10 12 14 16
VOGUE CO
4302
$1.25
Canada $1.35
Butterick
Instant Fashion Patterns
SIZE 8
SEW & GO
A knits-only wrap dress
1011
Size 12
Simplicity PRINTED Pattern
udella
SIZES 10 12 14 16 97cm
BUST 83 87 92
5889
A Multi-size Printed Pattern
VOGUE COUTURIER DESIGN
VOGUE COUTURIER DESIGN
Style
1568
$1.40 New Zealand
$1.80 Australia
Size 12
Bust 87 cm (34")
Miss

SEWING WITH AND WITHOUT PATTERNS

Sewing patterns provide you with a template to make one garment or a collection of variations of that garment. You can buy them online or in stores, or from the designers.

COMMERCIAL SEWING PATTERNS

The major sewing pattern companies offer a huge range of garment styles, and patterns at low prices come sales time. While they do have younger ranges, the designs tend to be aimed at an older market, and the ease added to a pattern is often generous. Instructions are fairly minimal, aimed at people who are already confident in their sewing. But hey, that's you now, *non*?

INDIE SEWING PATTERNS

A growing number of independent designers are publishing their patterns. The styles tend to be aimed at a more niche market, such as women with a particular body shape, vintage lovers, modern hipsters, or men. While the price of independent patterns is higher, they offer great value for money in terms of more detailed instructions and beautiful packaging. Take a look at my own line of stylish, wearable, and simple-to-use patterns at tillyandthebuttons.com.

DIGITAL SEWING PATTERNS

While many patterns come preprinted, some are offered as a digital file to download and print at home (or the office—ssshh!). You stick the individual pages together with glue or tape to form a full-size pattern sheet—this is easy to do and should only take about 20 minutes. Digital patterns may not have the beautiful packaging of their preprinted counterparts, and they do take a bit of extra effort, but on the plus side they are instant and cheaper to buy. Many indie pattern designers start sharing via digital.

VINTAGE SEWING PATTERNS

For a piece of sewing history, hunt down vintage sewing patterns on the Internet, in charity stores, and in specialty stores. With fashions from the 1920s (or earlier) through to the 1980s, the cover artwork ranges from the sublimely beautiful to the frankly quite disturbing! You may simply enjoy collecting the patterns as curiosities, but if you want to make the garment, be aware that there are a few differences from modern patterns. Vintage patterns often come in a single size rather than multiple sizes, the proportions will be different to reflect the typical body shape of the time or corsetry, they may have hole-punched rather than printed markings, and the instructions are often very vague, as more people knew how to sew in the olden days!

FREESTYLE SEWING

A pattern is a seriously useful template for creating clothing, but you don't necessarily need one. Some people prefer to freestyle it, either copying clothes that already fit them, making up their own patterns, or a combination of the two. A good place to start is www.diy-couture.co.uk.

REFASHIONING

You don't have to begin with a piece of flat fabric. Try breathing new life into clothes you don't wear anymore or repurposing a thrift store find. Use the techniques you've learned in this book to alter the fit and add embellishment details.

FURTHER READING AND RESOURCES

There's always more to learn, so here are a few suggestions to get you started.

BOOKS

***DIY COUTURE* by Rosie Martin (Laurence King, 2012)** A refreshingly simple approach to making clothes without patterns.

***FABRIC FOR FASHION: THE SWATCH BOOK* by Clive Hallett and Amanda Johnston (Laurence King, 2010)** Get a feel for different fabrics with over 100 swatches included.

***GERTIE'S NEW BOOK FOR BETTER SEWING* by Gretchen Hirsch (Stewart, Tabori & Chang, 2012)** A friendly introduction to couture sewing techniques.

***ME AND MY SEWING MACHINE* by Kate Haxell (Apple Press, 2010)** A beginner's guide to basic sewing techniques.

***SEW U: HOME STRETCH* by Wendy Mullin (Little, Brown, 2008)** Useful primer for overlocking and working with knit fabrics.

***THE COMPLETE BOOK OF SEWING* by Chris Jeffreys (Dorling Kindersley, 2006)** Handy guide to squillions of techniques.

***THE COMPLETE PHOTO GUIDE TO PERFECT FITTING* by Sarah Veblen (Creative Publishing International, 2012)** Detailed reference on altering patterns to fit your unique shape.

FABRIC

You can source fabric from specialty fabric stores (both online and offline), department stores, and markets. Most of the fabrics used in this book were supplied by:

RAY STITCH
www.raystitch.co.uk

THE FABRIC GODMOTHER
www.fabricgodmother.co.uk

THE VILLAGE HABERDASHERY
www.thevillagehaberdashery.co.uk

BLOGS

My blog, *tillyandthebuttons.com*, is bursting with many more tips, tutorials, and projects for making your own clothes.

There are thousands of other blogs out there where you can check out what talented DIY (do-it-yourself) dressmakers all over the world are creating. I read hundreds of blogs so it's hard to pick just a few, but these are some my favorites:

A STITCHING ODYSSEY
www.astitchingodyssey.com

DIBS AND THE MACHINE
www.missdibs.com

DID YOU MAKE THAT?
didyoumakethat.com

GINGERMAKES
gingermakes.wordpress.com

HANDMADE JANE
www.handmadejane.co.uk

HOUSE OF PINHEIRO
houseofpinheiro.blogspot.co.uk

JOLIES BOBINES
joliesbobines.wordpress.com

LAZY STITCHING
www.lazystitching.com

LLADYBIRD
lladybird.com

MY HAPPY SEWING PLACE
www.myhappysewingplace.com

NETTE
nettevivante.blogspot.co.uk

PAUNNET
www.paunnet.com

PENELOPING
peneloping.com

RUE DES RENARDS
ruedesrenards.wordpress.com

SO ZO . . . WHAT DO YOU KNOW?
sozowhatdoyouknow.blogspot.co.uk

SOWN BROOKLYN
sownbrooklyn.com

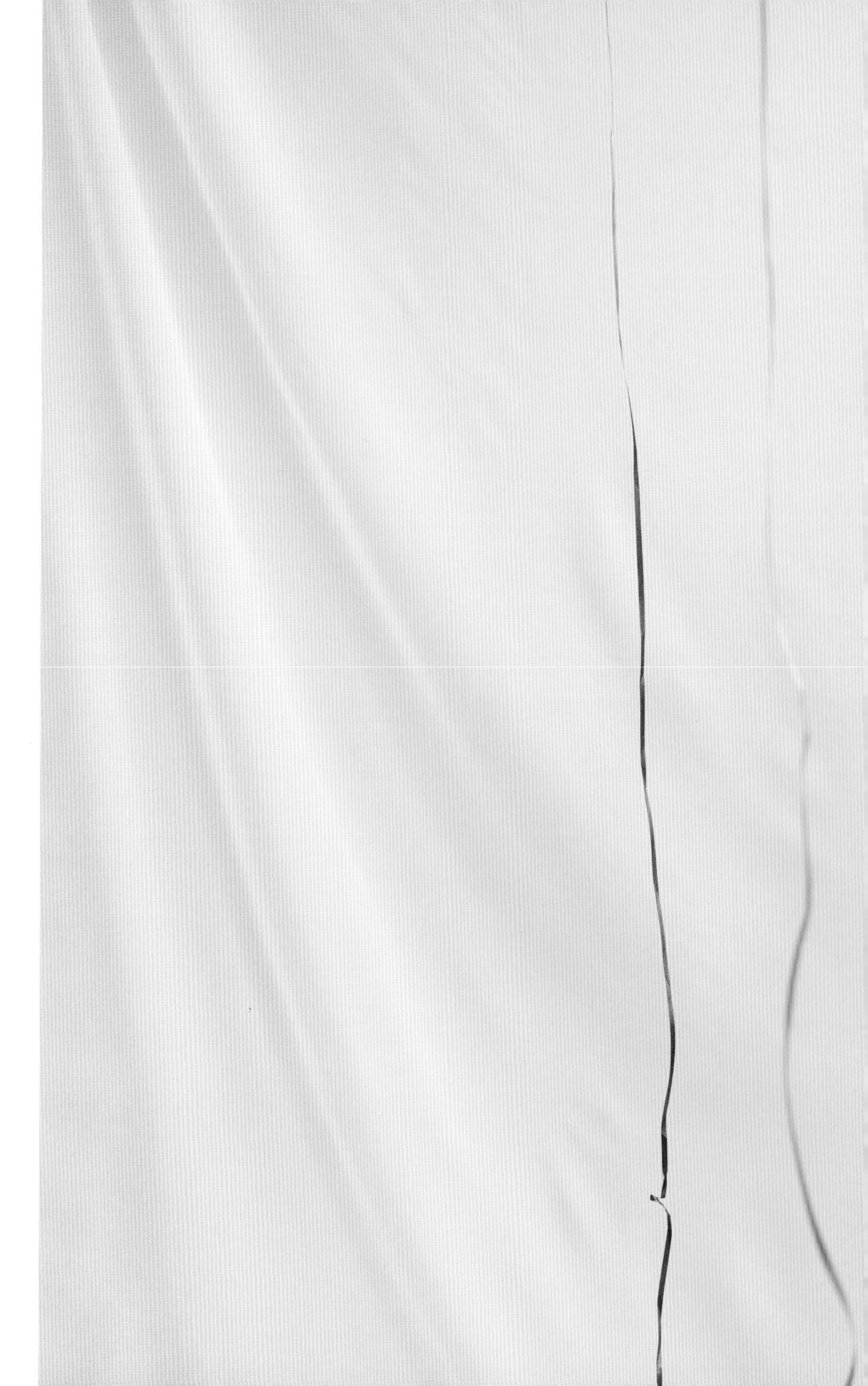

INDEX

DRESS

THANK YOU!

It may have my name on the front, but this book was in fact a team effort. Thank you, thank you, thank you . . .

To my amazing literary agent Marigold Atkey for doing such a brilliant job championing the book. Big thanks also to Lizzy Kremer, Petra Johnsson, and the team at David Higham Associates. I am also grateful to Rachel Khoo for making the introduction.

To Lisa Pendreigh for commissioning my first book, being so supportive, and basically making my dreams come true.

To Kate Haxell for your thoughtful editing and for putting me at ease during my first foray into the world of publishing.

To Arielle Gamble for your magical combination of creative talent and diligence that has made this book look so amazing, and for all the giggles behind the scenes.

To Ellie Smith for the gorgeous photos, Charlotte Melling for your creative eye (and for getting Breton stripes on the cover), Terri Capon for the gorgeous makeup 'n' hair, and Alex Davenport for your helping hands.

To Jane O'Shea, Helen Lewis, Ed Griffiths, Yvonne Doolan, Margaux Durigon, and everyone at Quadrille Publishing who worked on the original UK edition of the book.

To the wonderful pattern testers for your generosity, wisdom, and discerning eyes—Debi Fry, Joanna Furniss, Marie Koupparis, Mai Lin Li, Jane Marland, and Sarah Walter.

To Annie Barker at the Village Haberdashery, Rachel Hart at Ray Stitch, and Josie Hawes at Fabric Godmother for kindly supplying the beautiful fabrics used in the book.

To Fiona Douglas for giving me my first sewing lesson. It worked.

To my mum, dad, bro' Joe, and all my family and friends for cheering me along and for putting up with me being a troglodyte for so long. Special mentions to James Emmott for daring me to start a blog, Sara Robinson for asking the right questions, Zoe Edwards for the Strategy Meetings, Lauren Guthrie for always phoning at just the right time, and Sarah Cunliffe for never complaining about the thread all over the carpet. Extra special thanks to James Goddard for the supportive words and amazing back rubs.

Last but not least, I'd like to thank all the awesome people who read my blog for inspiring and encouraging me to continue doing what I do. You've made me a very happy lady, and I couldn't have done this without you.

Publishing Director Jane O'Shea
Commissioning Editor Lisa Pendreigh
Project Editor Kate Haxell
Creative Director Helen Lewis
Designer and Illustrator Arielle Gamble
Fashion Photography Ellie Smith
Styling Charlotte Melling
Step Photography Arielle Gamble
Production Director Vincent Smith
Production Controller Sasha Hawkes

Roost Books
An imprint of Shambhala Publications, Inc.
Horticultural Hall
300 Massachusetts Avenue
Boston, Massachusetts 02115
roostbooks.com

First published in 2014 by
Quadrille Publishing Ltd.

10 9 8 7 6 5 4 3 2 1

Printed in China

Distributed in the United States by Penguin Random House LLC and in Canada by Random House of Canada Ltd.

Library of Congress Cataloging-in-Publication Data

Walnes, Tilly
Love at first stitch: demystifying dressmaking / Tilly Walnes
Pages cm
Originally published: London: Quadrille Publishing, Ltd., 2014.
Includes index.
ISBN 978-1-61180-234-4 (pbk.: alk. paper)
1. Tailoring (Women's) 2. Machine sewing. 3. Dressmaking. I. Title.
TT519.5.W35 2014
646.4—dc23
2014017161